FOREW

'The Griese Valley and Beyond' is a collection o͏͏ a-
ditions from an area steeped in history. This bc͏͏ ne
before, who have created that history. It is also a tribute to those who have recognised the value of this colourful past and have recorded it for the benefit of those generations to come.

This area is going though a period of great change. New housing estates are being built in our villages and new families are bringing new life into the area. We welcome these new-comers and hope they will take cognisance of the rich history of the area they now call home. The inspiration for this book resulted from the writings of John Duffy of Poplar Hall, Ballitore, who has recorded his own experience of growing up, working and living in the area and who had already researched and compiled a considerable amount of material from the area.

When John's writings were brought to the attention of some local people it gave rise to discussions on the colourful and rich history of which this area boasts. John had a dream of publishing a book on the history of the area and the newly formed Narraghmore Local History Group decided to support this idea and bring John's dream to fruition and so the idea for this book was born.

Apart from his own research and writings John enthused many others in the community to get involved in the project and spent many hours persuading various people to put pen to pen and recount their own memories of the area. His enthusiasm was infectious and his powers of persuasion were such that people who had never dreamed of writing took on the task of researching and writing various articles.

John would also like to thank his daughter Kathleen Duffy for her help in transcribing many of the articles onto disc. Many people have put in many hours of work researching and writing the various articles in this book. We must also thank KELT for their support of this project.

This book covers various aspects of our history, the social life and community spirit which has made this area so special, the sporting achievements of our many and varied clubs, the important role played by the local schools, the role of the church in our community and of course the rich tapestry that has made up the history of the area.

It is far from being a complete and comprehensive history. There are many stories still untold, many more gems to be uncovered. This, rather, is a snapshot of the life and times of 'The Griese Valley and Beyond'.

Seamus Byrne

Chairperson
Narraghmore Local History Group

CONTENTS

EDUCATION
Page No.

Schools of Narraghmore 7
St Laurence's School 11
The Glebe 14

HISTORICAL

Ancient Ballitore 16
Ancient Cross at Lipstown 18
Blackhall Castle 19
Community Spirit 20
Killeen Cormac 22
Moyle Abbey 24
Robbery at the Brewery 27
The Ballad of Mullaghmast 28
O'Connell at Mullaghmast 30
Mullaghmast Commemoration 31
The Rath of Mullaghmast 32
The Rebellion of 1798 33

HOLY WELLS

Blessed Well at Rathside 36
St John's Well - Davidstown 36
St Patrick's Well - Glassealy 37
The Drummer's Well 40

RELIGION

Ballymount Chapel 42
Cardinal Cullen 44
Parish Priests of Narraghmore 44
Church of the Holy Saviour - Narraghmore 48
The Mission 50
Opening Crookstown Chapel 52

THE GRIESE VALLEY

& BEYOND

Edited by
Barbara Sheridan

THE NARRAGHMORE LOCAL HISTORY GROUP

THE GRIESE VALLEY & BEYOND

First Edition

A catalogue record for this title can be obtained from the British Library.
see ISBN No. above the barcode

Front Cover painting by:
Anne O'Reilly

Printed in November 2003 by
Millbrook Press, Naas, Co. Kildare

Published by
Retsila Publications Ltd © 2003
12 Rosewood, Calverstown, Kilcullen, Co. Kildare

On behalf of
THE NARRAGHMORE LOCAL HISTORY GROUP

All rights reserved. No Part of this publication may be reproduced in any form or by any means, electronic or mechanical including photocopying or recording, or by any information storage or retrieval systems, without the permission of The Narraghmore Local History Group.

CONTENTS

SOCIAL LIFE
Page No.

Ballitore - A Quaker Village 55
Ballitore ICA 57
Ballitore Library 58
Ballitore Picture House 60
Card Playing 61
Copper Beach at Poplar Hall 64
Hickeys of Calverstown 66
Industry in the Parish 72
Mayo Exodus 75
Memories from Crookstown 81
Memories of a Life Well Lived .84
Narraghmore Credit Union 90
Narraghmore Group Water Scheme 91
Lord Edwards own Pipe Band .92
Reflections from Inchaquire 94
The Goathouse 96
The Little Theatre 97
The Threshing 99

SPORT

Ballitore Game Club 102
Camogie 104
Horseracing 110
MillCeltic 114
Narraghmore Football Team 116
Narraghmore Parish GAA 117
Sport in the Parish 122
St Laurence's Golf Society .126

PHOTOGRAPHS

From the Archives 126
Colour Selection 137

Cookstown N.S. 1933

An Early Postcard from Ballitore

The Schools of Narraghmore from 1825

By Hilary Healy

The school system in Narraghmore, along with the rest of Ireland, should be understood in terms of education thought, political undercurrents and the social upheaval of the times. The Penal Laws, which had started in the late 17th century, had made any kind of Catholic or Dissenter education illegal. Although repealed by Relief Acts in 1782, 1792 and 1793 they were remembered and fear of proselytising groups was strong. The outbreak of the French Revolution brought a threat of popular revolt. It became important to condition the lower classes so they could resist revolutionary propaganda. Control of schools seemed like a good way to do this. Hence the proposal to set up a system of schooling throughout the country. It was planned that the schools would be multi-denominational but this did not happen on the ground.

The national school system was set up in 1831 but it was not until 1855 that a national school was set up in Ballymount (Usk). A national school for girls was set up in Crookstown in the same year. Crookstown Boys are men-

Ballymount National School

EDUCATION

tioned in 1867, Old Grange in 1869 and Skerries in 1875. The Protestant national school was set up in Timolin shortly after this. In the early 1900s a "new revised programme" introduced a wide range of subjects in these schools, which included the three Rs, kindergarten, drawing, singing, elementary science, PE, cookery and laundry as obligatory subjects. However the inspectors' reports from 1912 onwards note poor sanitation, insufficient heat and lack of desks for half the pupils. However the report does note "the teachers work very earnestly and use intelligent methods in all the subjects and the pupils are bright and earnest and very interested in their work". (1918 report)

Prior to the national school most of the school-going population attended what were known as hedge schools, set up as an answer to the harsh Penal Laws. These were still very popular at the beginning of the 19th century. Contrary to popular belief they were not universally held in hedgerows. More often they were held in the simple residence of the master, or if he was an itinerant, in the house of one of the scholars. The curriculum was extensive. They were taught reading, writing and arithmetic, and often Latin and even Greek. Some of the pupils were destined for the continental seminaries of the Catholic Church.

In Kildare there were between 184 and 194 'pay schools', mostly hedge schools, catering for about 9,000 children, all held in buildings. About 505 attended schools in this area. About 320 were boys and probably 185 girls attended school. However the Census of 1821 shows that in this area 3,799 children were under five years and 3,920 were aged between five and 10 years of age.

A further 2,976 were aged 10-15 years. Furthermore, only about 40% attended on any one day, so schooling was very sporadic for most.

An educational survey of 1826 mentions three such schools in this area. In the village of Timolin a Protestant teacher by the name of J.Hawkins kept school. The schoolhouse of lime and stone was worth about £200 which meant it was a very fine house indeed by the standards of the time. This was built by public subscription. The record shows that 17 pupils were of the Established Church and 18 were Roman Catholics. A Catholic named Owen Finn also ran a school in the village and this school received subscriptions from the Kildare Place Society (a Protestant body). It had 37 Protestant children and between 81 and 91 Catholic children attending.

In Spratstown a school run by a Catholic master, William Gyves, had 75 children, 69 Catholic. They were taught in a mud cabin worth about £8 and the master received about £10 per annum. In Crookstown a school was held under a Catholic woman called Sarah Gore. Her school had 18 children, 14 Catholic. Conditions must have been poor- it is described as a thatched cabin worth about £2/10 shillings and she herself received about £4/10 shillings per annum.

In Usk there were three hedge schools, all run by Roman Catholics. All three were housed in buildings of stone and yellow clay. Michael Byrne received from 1/ 8d to 3/8d per quarter, which amounted to about £5 per year. He had about 25 children attending. John Grading charged from 2/2d to 4/4d which gave him an annual income of about £6. Perhaps parents paid more because it was a better building. It was valued at £8 compared with Byrne's house which was valued at £4. The third school was run by Henry Nowlan and had about 45 pupils. He received an income of between £11 and £12 per annum.

Comparing this to the conditions of the time it is worth noting that agriculture was in a slump due to the end of the Napoleonic Wars and with 950 families in this area dependent on agriculture their position was often precarious. A flax mill had been set up in Inchaquire, but the returns were poor with women earning less that 2d a day by spinning flax. Peasants hired themselves out as labourers for about 4d a day, so money for schooling was difficult to find.

The Quaker School in Ballitore, under the Master James White, had 37 pupils, all male, of mixed denominations. It was a private boarding school, founded in 1726. Maria Edgeworth, the liberal educator, was a visitor to the school and often painted by the river Griese. Edmund Burke, later famous, reported that he had paid £6 a quarter which was a huge sum in the 1700s. Mr White is reported as receiving an annual income of £1,350 and comparing this to the salaries of two teachers in Athy at this time, who received £169/10/- (female) and £200 (male) it is clear that his income was substantially higher. The pupils at the Quaker School were different to those attending other schools in the area. Many of them had aspirations to third level education and among the most famous pupils were Edmund Burke and Paul Cullen, later to become archbishop and then Cardinal Cullen.

It is clear there was quite a divide in the education systems in operation in this area. The quality of education offered was generally good, but given the economic circumstances of the time, few could avail of that on offer and fewer still could attend regularly. However compared to other areas of the country this locality was quite well catered for.

Pals outside Ballymount N.S.
Back Row: Kit Ward, Sean O'Neill, Joe McGrath, Pat O'Connor
Front Row: Mary Ward, Monica O'Connor, Maura Russell.

EDUCATION

CROOKSTOWN N.S. 1948

(left to right) Front row : Jamesy Swaine, Dessie Lynch, Anthony Fenlon, Mark Wright, Leo Reddy, Johnny Reilly, John Dempsey.

Second row: Sean Mc Loughlin, Tony Delaney, Tom Lambe, ?, Mick Higgins, Charlie Jones, Joe Delaney, Harold Mc Loughlin.

Third row: ?, ?, ?, Mick Lawlor, Eugene Callaghan, Donald Doyle, Paddy Wright, ?, Anthony Archibald, ?, ?, Larry Swaine.

Fourth row: Joe Dempsey, Jimmy Russell, Anthony Delaney, Tom Kelly, Paddy O'Halloran, Liam Kelly, Sean O'Gorman.

Fifth row: Charlie Timmons, Jim Mc Loughlin, Paddy Scully, ?, Christy Higgins, Mel Lynch, Danno Mackey, Mick Kane.

Teachers: Mr Crowley and Mr Tansey.

St Laurence's National School 1960s to Present Day

By Carmel Gleeson

As far as we know the boys and girls of Crookstown were in the original buildings from the time of the founding of the national school system until the new school, St Laurence's was built in the 1960s.

Originally there were two schools, one for the boys and one for the girls, located where Crookstown Parish Hall (i.e. the Little Theatre) now stands. Mr Michael Fahey was principal of the boys' school and Mrs Owens was in charge of the girls'. These two schools and Ballymount National School where the principal was Mr Sam Sloan, were amalgamated, giving rise to the present St Laurence's NS which was built on a site given by Mr Michael Kerwin. The school opened in 1968 with Mr Sloan as principal.

As the school population continued to grow there was a demand for more facilities and another new building, comprised of two classrooms, a general-purpose room, staff room and kitchen, was opened in 1977, replacing the prefab.

In 1975 the first boards of management were appointed to all primary schools. Up to this time the parish priest was manager. From 1971 to 1975 Fr James Brophy was manager of the school. After his death he was replaced by Fr Henry O'Connor, the new parish priest who was chairperson until his death in 1998. The present chairperson is Fr Vincent Dempsey, PP. Paddy Murphy of Blackhall, served as chairman for the school year 2001-2002 during Fr Dempsey's year in California and Israel.

Father Brophy made big staffing changes in the school shortly after his arrival. He appointed four new teachers, all raw recruits from the training colleges. These new teachers were TJ Barry, Carmel Morley, Bridget Sweeney and Carmel Gallagher (now Carmel Gleeson, present principal). Carmel Morley stayed for one year and was replaced by local girl Pauline Doyle from Mullaghmast. Pauline (now Whelan) is principal of the girls' school in Portarlington, County Laois.

Sam Sloan continued as principal until 1990 when he retired and was replaced by Carmel Gleeson, then vice-principal.

The school continued to grow in size and by the mid '80s there were eight teachers and an administrative principal on the staff.

After much campaigning a remedial teacher was appointed in 1991. This teacher is on the staff of St Laurence's NS but also teaches two days a week in Scoil Ide, Kilmead, the other parish school.

EDUCATION

IN 1994 the Minister for Education at the time, Niamh Breathnach, officially opened another new building, comprised of a new remedial classroom and toilets funded by the department and local fundraising and an additional classroom sponsored by the Fahey family in memory of their deceased parents. Mr Michael Fahey had taught and been principal of Crookstown boys' school for many years.

Presentation of Plaque 1994

In 1999 a very active parents' council persuaded the then Minister for Education Micheál Martin to visit the school to discuss staffing. In recent years the school has erected a prefab, with two additional classrooms and a principal's office.

St Laurence's NS continues to grow with many new housing developments in the parish.

There have been corresponding changes in the personnel. September 2003 saw 12 teachers on the staff, nine class teachers, Maria Downey (Deputy Principal), Geraldone Hoban, Claire Harvey-Burgess, Noreen Forrest, Moira Liddane, Marie Hill, Breege Buchs, Imy O'Donovan and Jacqueline Ward. Jacqueline is a past pupil of the school.

In October staff and parents were sorry to see Marie Hill heading back to Tralee after being 17 years on the staff. Marie has been replaced by Kathy Roche. Special needs are catered for by the Learning Support Teacher, Hilary Healy and Resource Teacher, Sally Ann Bell. Carmel Gleeson is now an administrative principal. New innovations in staffing have meant that Claire Harvey-Burgess and Breege Buchs could take up job-sharing so the school has a temporary teacher, Sandra O'Brien. Also on the school staff at present are Erin Byrne, Special Needs Assistant, Rosemary Devereux, secretary, Sharon Mulhall, caretaker, Rosario Corcoran and Ann Swayne, cleaning ladies.

In 1991 the school affiliated to the newly formed Cumann na mBunscol and this was the start of a most successful sporting era. As well as its many academic successes, St Laurence's NS now has many sporting achievements to its credit, culminating in the Leinster Leader School of the Year award in 1997.

Over the years the school has welcomed many distinguished visitors. These included GAA presidents Jack Boothman and Sean McCague, Mick O'Dwyer, many of the Kildare senior football team, Kilkenny camogie players Angela and Ann Downey and basketball player Michelle Aspell. Many of the school's pupils have been selected to play in Croke Park in camogie and Gaelic games.

EDUCATION

St. Laurence's School Band 1984

Boys from St. Laurence's N.S. who won the Mini-Sevens in Gaelic Football 1998
Back Row (L to R): John Fogarty, Liam Treacy, Padraig Kearney, JP Byrne.
Front Row: Andrew Ward, Sean Higgins, Dessie Lawlor, Stephen Hickey, David Ging, Padraig O'Neill

EDUCATION

The Glebe - Crookstown

By Sheila Whelan

The Glebe - formerly The 'Narraghmore Parochial School and Garden'

A plaque that hangs in Narraghmore Church tells the tragic tale of the untimely death in 1840 of 18-year-old Henry Torrens, youngest son of Venerable John Torrens, DD, Archdeacon of Dublin and Rector of Narraghmore.

The plaque originally hung on the gable of the Glebe schoolhouse in Crookstown which was built by his family in his memory and was probably moved when the church body sold the property. The plaque does not give an exact date of when the building was erected but it was between 1840 and 1885.

The earliest documentation of the building refers to the Educational Endowments (Ireland) Act of 1885 and the caretakers of the building were named as "The Dublin, Glendalough and Kildare Diocesan Board of Education". The school is named as "Narraghmore Parochial School and Garden, in County Kildare in the Barony of Narragh and Reban East,

EDUCATION

(with the adjoining land comprising 1 acre, 3 roods and 17 perches or thereabouts). The owners recorded are the Representative Church Body.

There is said to have been a chapel and schoolroom on either end of the building and what is believed to have been a teacher's living quarters upstairs. The building is shown on a map as a chapel of ease but it is not confirmed if it was used as a church.

Although there is no reference in the deeds of a change of use or ownership the house was used as a Catholic secondary school in the early '50s. A Miss M Brophy from Paulstown, Kilkenny founded it and Miss Annie Brennan, a niece of Miss Annie Lavin, then postmistress of Ballitore and a cousin of Charlie Lavin, Ballitore, taught in the school. A local retired national schoolteacher Mrs O'Connor, aunt of Pat O'Connor, Ballitore, taught singing and music. It was called the Secondary School of Our Lady of Loretto. At any given time there were about 40 pupils enrolled. It was a private school with fees of nine guineas per year. There were two classrooms, one at either end of the building. The students sat their Intermediate and Leaving Certificate exams in the Convent of Mercy School in Athy. The school closed in or about 1960/61.

The Church of Ireland's Education Board sold the building in October 1972 to a lady by the name of Margaret Kingsbury, otherwise Margaret Gregson. As Narraghmore School was no longer used as a school due to the rationalisation scheme introduced by the Department of Education some times previously whereby smaller schools in country areas were closed and the pupils sent to the larger schools in nearby towns, the diocesan board indicated that as it was no longer required as a school the most beneficial way of dealing with the property was to sell it.

The board had to apply to the Commissioners of Charitable Donations and Bequests for Ireland to seek permission to sell the property.

Later documents refer to Mrs Josephine Gregson as the owner. We assume this to be the daughter of Margaret Gregson, although this cannot be confirmed.

Other listed owners of the property are Paul Klann 1974-1976. The building became known as 'The Gables' at this time.

James Brennan and Helen Kehoe lived there with their young family from 1979 to 1986.

The present owners Larry and Sheila Whelan purchased the house on paper as 'The Gables' but local people referred to it as 'The Glebe'. They prefer this name and have returned to using this title but have no record of its origin.

I would like to acknowledge the following who helped to gather the information for this article: John Duffy, Lily Foley, a past pupil of the school, Charlie Lavin and Mrs and Mrs Willie Neill.

HISTORICAL

ANCIENT BALLYTORE

by
John Whelan (Jack the Poet)

In smiling June when flowers bloom,
Bedecked each meadow gay,
Along the banks of the river Griese,
I carelessly did stray,
To view the flowers with snowy fleece,
Whilst the lark on high did soar,
In rapture there I stood and gazed on ancient Ballytore,

The trout were nimbly sporting,
Along the silvery brook,
The angler slowly strolled along with deceitful fly and hook,
As the milkmaid tripped she oe'r the plain,
Her vocals she did power,
Which made the air swell with song, surrounding Ballytore.

The labourers to their daily toil,
Were beginning to appear,
The chapel bell the breeze did swell,
As it summoned them to prayer,
With uplifted hands and fervent hearts,
Their maker to implore,
To bless the earth that gave them birth, near ancient Ballytore,

The rose upon its thorny throne,
Had not dislodged the morning dew,
The modest daisy with its tinged leaves,
Displayed a crimson hue,
Across the plain the feathered train,
Did join in one harmonious corps,
In a thrilling blaze of celestial praise, oe'r ancient Ballytore.

Being elevated by these charming scenes,
I grew more eager still,
With hearty steps I did advance,
To view the noble mill,
To see each industrious hand at work,
Whilst machinery did roar,
By the surge of the river Griese that flows through Ballytore.

HISTORICAL

Frenchpark, Willowbrook, and Greece Mount, ,
are enclosed by shady groves,
Where the cheerful youth of that brave town,
For recreation goes,
There the nimble bee sweeps oe'r the plain,
And from each flower extracts their store,
To lay it up for winter, near ancient Ballytore.

To describe the beauties of fair Oakfield,
On you I need not call,
Since Kavanagh in his oration,
Declared it outshined them all,
Its splendid dwellings and flowery shades,
The sway it always bore,
It embelishes each poets laye, on ancient Ballytore.

When bright soul sends forth its golden rays,
It would your heart delight,
To see the splendour of that tranquil town,
And its far famed school of white,-
It was to this school great Edmund Burke,
First came to seek lore,
With hundreds of other noble youths, to ancient Ballytore.

Though neglected noble prospect stands,
yet I cannot forget,
It was here blessed Cardinal Cullen,
First drew infant breath,
The first Prince of the Roman Church,
A Cardinal's hat he wore,
Of which no other town can boast, but ancient Ballytore.

Some religious piles of ancient styles,
Stood near this handsome town,
Till by the Puritans they were wrecked,
And leveled to the ground,-
St Patrick of Glasealy,
with ancient Narraghmore,
Moyle Abbey on the River Griese, that flows through Ballytore.

Wicklow may boast of Glendalough,
With her romantic scene.
Kerry of Killarney,
And Meath of lofty scenes,
Cork of Castle Blarney,
Kilkenny on the Nore,
In second there Kildare can boast of Ancient Ballytore.

HISTORICAL

Ancient cross at Lipstown

By John Duffy

In a field at Lipstown, three-quarters of a mile to the east of Narraghmore village, an ancient cross stands on the summit of the high ground in a square, unenclosed plot which is never tilled like the rest of the field. This plot is probably the site of a long-forgotten burial ground as skulls and bones have been turned up close by.

The cross is inserted in a rough limestone flag. It is in one piece and measures 6' 2" in height. The head is ringed but the stone is not pierced through. What is unusual is that the front and back of the cross are much narrower than the sides; the breadth of the former is 7.5", while the sides are as much as 13". There is a tradition that many years ago an attempt was made to remove the cross to Kilcullen. It was brought as far as the eastern 'ditch' of the 'cross-field' but beyond that it could not be stirred and tradition states that the next morning it was found back in its original location.

The Cross at Lipstown

HISTORICAL

Blackhall Castle

By Naomi White

Blackhall Castle is located approximately two miles between the two villages of Calverstown and Narraghmore.

Built in the early part of the 15th century it was occupied by the Eustace family, of Ballymore-Eustace fame. John Fitzmaurice of Blackhall was High Sheriff in 1400 and 1402. He was one of 12 people chosen to control the defences of Kildare in 1404.

In 1576 Robert Wellesley lived in Blackhall. He passed the property to his son Gerald and it is known that in 1620 Richard Wellesley held 460 acres of land attached to the castle. Nothing remains today of any of the Eustace's properties or estates, except Blackhall Castle. The castle contains a sheelah-na-gig, a carved stone of a nude female figure. It is thought that these carvings are associated with fertility and the belief in the evil eye. It is also believed to be the only one in County Kildare.

In January 1999 half of the castle collapsed after a prolonged spell of bad weather but, due to the help of an emergency grant, the castle has now been rendered safe and hopefully no more deterioration will occur.

It is privately owned and is open to the public for two and a half months each year.

On the set of King Arthur - Ballymore Eustace 2003

HISTORICAL

Community spirit in 1914

Down through the years many people have played important roles in the local community. Their dedication and work has been recognised and it is customary to honour them with a presentation.

A presentation to one such person in 1914 is well documented and is worthy of publication to demonstrate the strong community spirit in the area in the past.

The person to be honoured was Dr M Kenna, Blackrath, coroner for South Kildare and for almost 30 years, medical officer of the district. A meeting was called by Rev Mr McGee on Monday March 9, 1914 at 11am.

The object of the meeting, which was attended by a number of local people and clergy, was to form a committee for the purpose of making a presentation to Dr Kenna. It was decided to open a subscription list and to have circulars printed, giving a list of subscriptions promised at the meeting and of other subscriptions promised afterwards.

The subscriptions were collected and the committee continued to meet. By June 15 that year the subscriptions collected amounted to £665 and it was decided to leave the fund open for two more weeks as more funds had been promised. It was decided, along with the cash presentation, to present the good doctor with an illuminated address, which was not to cost more than £10!

The following is a copy of the address and presentation made to Dr Kenna.

"We, representing many of your friends, irrespective of creed, politics or station in life, not only those living in Ireland but also many who live in England, Scotland, Rome and the Colonies, to whom, as to us, you endeared yourself by your many acts of kindness and by your unfailing courtesy, desire to congratulate you on your having attained to almost 30 years of service as medical officer of this district.

"The names attached to this address bear eloquent testimony to the love and esteem in which you are held by all, high and low, rich and poor alike. You have endeared yourself to those amongst whom you have laboured for so many years, by your self-sacrificing devotion to duty, whenever the call came, in the morning, at noon-day, or at night, you were always ready and willing to respond.

"Your success as a highly qualified practitioner inspired confidence in your patients and made them feel that they could entirely trust to your judgement as well as to your devotion to their case. Your kindness to, and consideration for, the poor has long been a household word, and the universal feeling amongst them is that they shall not look upon your like again. Your appointment as Coroner for South Kildare was a fitting recognition of your success as a practitioner and of your high qualities as a man of sound judgement.

"Praying that god may long spare you to work amongst us, and asking your acceptance of the accompanying purse of 680 sovereigns as a total of our respect and esteem."

Fr. James Conway with his old school friend Piper Jack O'Connor on the occasion of the 50th anniversary in the priesthood at Crookstown Church.

HISTORICAL

Killeen Cormac

By John Duffy

Killeen Cormac lies three miles northeast of Ballitore in the townland of Colbinstown, Barony of Narragh and Reban, County Kildare. The site of this old cemetery is in a valley of the most picturesque character. The River Griese flows through the valley, separating the counties of Kildare and Wicklow at Killeen Cormac. In the valley there are many isolated mounds or eskers, retaining names connected with the legends and history of the area.

On the left bank of the Griese, in the parish of Ballynure, is a long esker called "Bullock Hill". On the opposite bank, on the Kildare side, is another esker called "Crocbunnion". To the west of this is another elevation, the highest of the group. On its summit is a rath of large proportions and at its base flows a small stream known as the "Scrughan", which joins the Griese, west of Killeen. This hill is called Rathownbeg. Between this and Knockbunnion is another esker of oval shape lying on a north south axis. This is Killeen Cormac. It was enclosed with a stone wall and trees were planted around the mound. The whole enclosure is occupied with graves, and on the summit is an oblong depression, the site of an early church.

The outline of three terraces, which surround the esker, can be traced. Within this enclosure are some pillar stones with Ogham inscriptions; one of these has an incised bust of the Redeemer. Another has a well-defined Ogham inscription carried around its top and sides. Killeen Cormac was used as a pagan burial ground before the introduction of Christianity. The pillar stones, some with Oghan inscriptions, placed at intervals around the base of the tumulus, reminds me very much of the burial Tumuli on the Boyne and other well-known places.

On the lowest side of the mound there is another pillar stone. On its top surface there is a mark which is supposed to represent a hound's paw. As this stone is the subject of a very curious legend it deserves a mention. Local tradition, with a view perhaps to account for the name of the cemetery, tells that this stone marks the grave of Cormac, King of Munster. He was borne to this cemetery by a team of bullocks that were allowed to follow their own instincts in bearing the body of Cormac, for which rival claims were made, to his grave. Tradition states that he was carried from a long distant place, from the direction of Timolin, and that when the team reached the "Doon" of Ballynure the bullocks were overcome with thirst. They pawed the ground from which burst forth a spring of water. This still flows by the side of the road, opposite Donoghue's. The bullocks, having taken the water thus provided, travelled on until they came

HISTORICAL

to "Bullock Hill" opposite the cemetery. At this place they stood and refused to move any further.

From this it was apparent that Killeen was to be the last resting place of Cormac. The team of bullocks, having crossed the stream, left the body for burial in the cemetery. They turned for home across the marsh between the cemetery and "Bullock Hill". While crossing the Griese they were swept away and lost forever.

Another version of the legend tells that there was a hound on the team with the corpse, when it halted at "Bullock Hill". The hound jumped across the river to the cemetery and, alighting on the top of the pillar stone, impressed the mark of his paw, thus indicating the precise spot where Cormac was to be laid. Killeen Cormac was used by local families as their burialground until recent times. During the year Mass was celebrated for all those interred there and the graveyard was cleaned up.

For further information on Killeen Cormac read St. Patrick or Loca Patriciana by Rev. J. F. Shearman, CC Publisher, M H Gill and Son 1882.

The bodies of the men who died at Pike Bridge in 1798 were buried on this tree crowned Hillock near Crookstown, Ballitore, Co. Kildare

HISTORICAL

MOYLE ABBEY

By Andrew Forrest

The town land of Moyle Abbey is in south Kildare in the parish of Narraghmore. The old burial ground is about 100 yards from the N9 on your right as you drive towards Dublin, midway between Castledermot and Kilcullen. The remains of old walls and foundations cover an area of five or six acres, all of which are now covered with a layer of soil and grass. Down through the years the upper walls were carted away by local farmers to build roads and houses.

All the experts on these matters agree that Moyle Abbey was a Christian settlement long before St Patrick came to Ireland. We are a little uncertain about the exact date of the coming of these early Christians, they more than likely were fleeing to a place of safety from the Romans who were, at that time, throwing Christians to the lions to keep themselves amused.

On November 23, 1972, I was walking along by the little stream which rises from the 'Monk's Well'. It flows past the burial ground, right at the foot of the wall that surrounds the graveyard. As I walked past I saw what looked like a human bone. I pulled away some long grass and there it was - a human rib cage.

I went home to get some handy tools knowing that the task ahead would be difficult as it was obvious the person had not been properly buried. Needless to say bones lying on top of the ground will become very fragile.

Kilgowan Stone found by Willie Kelly (R.I.P.) in 1986

HISTORICAL

It appeared as if this person fell dead while stepping over the little stream. The upper part of the body must have decayed away on the dry bank while there was no trace whatever of that part of the body which fell in the stream.

As I probed the dry bank I came upon a few bones that crumbled into dust, but later I found bones that kept their shape and I put these in a box. I then investigated further and in a little space I found the skull.

This was like old times in Egypt in the 1930s when I spent all my spare time working with Sir Alec Locknee at various digs around the step pyramid at Sacara and elsewhere.

Now I had the skull in my hand, it looked normal and I was a little disappointed. When I turned it over I saw a round hole in the side of the skull which led me to believe this man was killed in battle by a blow from a sword or battle axe. I put it in the box with the other bones.

Feeling in some way responsible for this unfortunate man who had never been properly buried I set out next morning to meet Fr Jennings who was curate in this parish at that time.
I asked him to offer Mass for a poor man who had never been buried. "What is his name" asked Fr Jennings and I told him the whole story. He said he would come up to Moyle Abbey later and we would give the remains a Christian burial. I forgot to mention that I had already contacted the gardaí and the coroner.

After examining the bones the coroner said they were several hundred years old. On hearing this the gardaí said they had no further interest as 20 years was their limit. When Fr Jennings arrived at Moyle Abbey we examined the skull again and decided the right thing to do was to take the bones to the National Museum where a proper examination could be carried out.

The museum told us we would have a full report in a few day's time. In the meantime I had to supply every scrap of information regarding the 'find'.
Three weeks later I received Professor Erskine's report which indicated that the skull found was that of a male aged 40-50 years. The condition of the skull suggested a medieval date. According to Professor Erskine "the opening in this skull was made during life and the individual survived for more than one year, probably several years. It was not caused by disease processes or accidental trauma. It can be concluded that this opening is a trepanation".

Subsequently everything was carefully packed and Fr Jennings was instrumental in bringing them to the notice of Professor Raftery, Keeper of Irish Antiquities in UCD who had expressed great interest in the find, it being possibly the oldest example of successful trepanation so far discovered in this country.

The bones were discovered slightly more than four inches beneath the surface. This added to the difficulty of removing them in their utterly fragile condition, owing to the penetration of

HISTORICAL

the surrounding soil by brier and grass roots.

From the professor's report we know that the remains which I found were on that bank for 600-700 years. This would lead me to conclude that by 1272 nothing remained of the religious community which occupied Moyle Abbey. Had the monks still lived at Moyle Abbey we can take it for granted no human being would have been left to be feasted upon, providing food for grey crows and water rats.

Since I informed the National Museum of Ireland of my discovery and also about two bullaun stones at Moyle Abbey we have had many experts come to examine them.

The bigger of the two stones is in the graveyard, no doubt placed there many years ago by thoughtful people who felt the stone was important from an historical point of view. The second, smaller, stone is probably more interesting. One day I happened to meet up with a geologist who was doing a survey of the stone types available in these countries. He quickly identified that the first stone was made from granite which is readily available in Wicklow and Kildare.

The other stone which I had removed from the middle of a field and placed in our garden for safe keeping, presented more of a challenge. Dr Neville was unable to make a guess as to where it had come from originally. It is not granite, nor is it limestone or sandstone, and it was not indigenous to this country. It is extremely heavy for its size and is pinkish or wine coloured and it is most likely that the original refugees from Italy or Northern Europe brought this stone with them to Moyle Abbey where they prospered in peace for hundreds of years.

Then a new enemy, the Danes made Dublin their HQ and Moyle Abbey was within striking distance. It is possible Moyle Abbey came under attack from time to time. Numbers dwindled and with no new recruits from Europe it became more difficult for Moyle Abbey to survive as a religious settlement.

It is agreed by all experts on early Christianity that these bullaun stones were associated with the very early Christian church and it is believed that surplus consecrated wine was poured into the hollow in the stones and allowed to seep into the ground. The stone protected the area and prevented people walking over or disrespecting the holy place in any way.

From time to time we had many visitors wishing to examine the stone in our garden. Among them was a man from Pennsylvania, USA who said his church would pay a large sum for such a stone connected with early Christianity. I told him I did not regard myself as the owner of the stone, merely its caretaker.

Years ago the late Miss Polly Byrne, who was then owner of the field in the middle of which stood the smaller stone, told me how a priest in Crookstown offered to take the stone to the church for safe keeping but this did not happen and she was worried that it would be stolen. She asked me to take the stone for safe-keeping. I had it in our garden for years. One day I invited Fr Dempsey, PP, to have a look at the stone. To my surprise he knew more about these stones than I did myself.

When I asked him to take the stone to Crookstown church for safe keeping he was delighted to offer help. A few days later Edward O'Mara and Kevin Mooney arrived with a car and trailer and together they took the stone to Crookstown Church. Thanks to Fr Dempsey the stone is back on holy ground once more after centuries in the wilderness. Let us hope and pray that here it will be safe for another 2000 years.

Robbery at the Brewery

By John Duffy

In Crookstown down by the banks of the river Griese, about 200 yards from the overflow, are the old ruins of a building which was once a brewery. It dates back to the 17th century. There was a robbery in the brewery during which a life was lost. The stolen money was hidden in the gates of Poplar Hall.

In Penal days when Mass was celebrated at Croiceanaifren, not far from the brewery where the robbery took place, Fr O'Rourke spoke to the people at Mass about the robbery. He said while one life was lost during the robbery, two would be lost at the finding of the money, so the money was never found.

A woman by the name of Keating was involved in the robbery. When she died she was refused burial in a graveyard. Initially she was to be buried in Byrne's Church Yard, which is where the garda barracks in Ballitore is located today. However she was also refused burial here and she was finally interred in Cole's field in Inchaquire. A large rock marks the spot in the corner of the field.

HISTORICAL

BALLAD OF
MULLAGHMAST

by
By RD. Williams.

O'er the Rath of Mullaghmast,
On the solemn midnight blast,
What bleeding spectres passed,
With their gashed breasts bare?
Hast thou heard the fitful wail
That o'erloads the sullen gale,
When the waning moon shines pale
O'er the cursed ground there?

Hark hollow moans arise
Through the black tempestuous skies,
and curses, strife, and cries,
From the lone Rath swell;
For bloody Sydney there
Nightly fills the lurid air
With the unholy pomp and glare
Of the foul, deep hell.

He scorches up the gale
With his knights, in fiery mail;
And the banners of the Pale
O'er the red ranks rest.
But a wan and gory band
All apart and silent stand,
And they point th' accusing hand
At the hell-hound's crest!

HISTORICAL

Red streamlets, trickling slow,
O'er their clotted clothing flow,
And still and awful woe
On each pale brow weeps.
Rich bowls bestrew the ground,
And broken Harps abound
Whose once enchanting sound
In the bard's blood sleeps.

False Sydney! knighthood's stain,
The trusting brave in vain -
Thy guests ride o'er the plain
To thy dark cow're snare.
Flow'r of Offaly and Leix,
They have come thy board to grace
Fools to meet a faith less race
Save with true swords bare.

While cup and song abound,
The triple lines surround
The closed and guarded mound,
In the night's dark noon.
Alas! too brave O'More,
Ere the revelry was o'er
They have spilled thy young heart's gore,
Snatched from love too soon.

Though the Saxon snake unfold
At thy feet his scales of gold,
And vow thee love untold,
Trust him not, Green Land!

HISTORICAL

Daniel O'Connell at Mullaghmast

By Lorraine Callaghan

AN estimated 800,000 people, 10 times the number of people who attended the All Ireland football final in Croke Park in 2003, gathered at the Rath of Mullaghmast on Sunday, October 1,1843, for the monster Repeal Meeting addressed by the Liberator Daniel O'Connell in favour of annulling the Union with England.

Plans for the massive meeting had been ongoing in the area in the weeks prior to the meeting. Local people built a large platform in the meeting field which adjoined the Rath field and a Mr Fagan from Athy erected a huge pavilion. A banquet was held in this pavilion after the meeting at which 700 people sat down to a hot meal, a major catering achievement even by today's standards.

En route to the meeting O'Connell's procession passed through Old Kilcullen, Calverstown, Halverstown, Blackhall and Narraghmore and onwards to the Rath of Mullaghmast. The roadsides were lined with cheering crowds along the whole route from Kilcullen.

Explaining why he had chosen Mullaghmast for the meeting O'Connell said: "At Mullaghmast, and I have chosen this for this obvious reason, we are on the precise spot where English treachery- aye and false Irish treachery too, consummated a massacre that has never been imitated, save in the massacre of the Mamelukes by Mahomet Ali. It was necessary to have Turks atrocious enough to commit a crime equal to that perpetuated by the Englishman. (Hear hear) But do not think the massacre at Mullaghmast was a question between Protestants and Catholics- it was no such thing. The murdered persons were, to be sure, Catholics, but a great number of the murderers were also Catholics and Irishmen, because they were then, as well as now, many Catholics who were traitors to Ireland. But we have now this advantage, that we may have many honest Protestants joining us, joining us heartily in hand and heart for old Ireland and liberty...

"Oh my friends I will keep you clear of all treachery, there shall be no bargains, no compromise with England. We shall take nothing but Repeal and a parliament in College Green near the statue of King Billy in College Green." O'Connell's speech was interspersed with loud cheers of support from the large gathering.

Mullaghmast Commemoration

By Lorraine Callaghan

The 150th anniversary of Daniel O'Connell's meeting at Mullaghmast took place on October 3, 1993. Daniel O'Connell's direct descendant, Professor Maurice O'Connell, unveiled an engraved granite boulder to mark the event. Willie Kelly and John O'Brien placed a time capsule, containing newspapers of 1993, which is not to be opened until the year 2093, in a specially constructed chamber in the base of the memorial.

A pageant was held re-enacting part of the 1843 meeting. Local people, Eugene Callaghan, John Donovan, PJ Willis, John Duffey, Jack Fleming, Jimmy Lawler, Margaret Blanchfield, Lorraine Callaghan and Chris Moore, with Kieran Rigney from Naas playing Daniel O'Connell, acted out the scene from 1843. The parade was led by the band of the Curragh Command and followed by the Narraghmore Pipe Band. Children from Timolin, Kilmeade and Crookstown schools were also involved in the pageant. There was ceol agus rince, organised by Margaret Timmons and provided by Kilmeade Irish Figure Dancers with music from the local Ceoltas group led by Joe Lanigan.

THE MULLAGHMAST PAGEANT

The Rath of Mullaghmast

By Lorraine Callaghan

The Rath of Mullaghmast is an Iron Age ringfort, situated on high ground to the west of Ballitore.

In ancient history it is referred to as 'Maistean', 'Rath Maistin', 'Mullagh Maistean', 'Maistui of the Kings' and other variations. These however have contracted to its present form of Mullaghmast (Mullagh Maistin) which means Maistin's Hill.

On New Year's Day 1577 the Seven Septs of Laois were summoned, together with many of the chieftains of Offaly, to the Rath of Mullaghmast. There they were attacked and 399 people were murdered.

That was 400 years ago and today the bloodholes are only a dimple in the ground, but at the time of the massacre they were said to be 20 feet deep. There are a number of accounts of the events of that day, all of which agree that there was indeed a massacre, that those who were killed were supposedly under the protection of their slayers and that all were killed in cold blood.

The following account is given in 'The Annals of the Four Masters' edited by Dr John O'Donovan.

"A horrible and abominable act of treachery was committed by the English of Leinster and Meath upon that part of the people of Offaly and Leix that remained in confederacy with them and under their protection. It was effected thus: They were all summoned to show themselves with the greatest number they could be able to bring with them, at the Rath of Mullach-Maistean; and on their arrival at that place they were surrounded on every side by four lines of soldiers and cavalry who proceeded to shoot and slaughter them without mercy, so that not a single individual escaped by flight or force."

Those murdered at Mullaghmast included some of the Seven Septs of Leix and some of the Keatings. The Seven Septs of Leix are; the O'Mores, the O'Kellys, the O'Lalors, the Devoys, the Macaboys, the O'Dorans and the O'Dowlings.

HISTORICAL

The Rebellion of 1798

On the morning of May 24 nine loyalists under John Jefferies, a yeoman sergeant, repulsed a rebel attack on Narraghmore courthouse led by Malachi Delaney and James Murphy, the attack lasted two hours. Afraid that their position was untenable, the loyalists proceeded to Jefferies' home but were driven out when the rebels set the house on fire. Three loyalists were killed and six, including Jefferies, were taken prisoner by the rebels who had rallied under Daniel Walsh.

Lt. Eadie and the detachment from Ballitore routed a party of rebels in the woods near the town where five loyalists had been hanged. Later, near Fonstown, troops under Major Montresor routed the rebels who retreated to Ballitore. Jefferies was lodged in Ballitore but escaped to Athy.

Pushing on towards Red Gap Hill, Montresor was joined by Captain Rudd and Lt. Eadie. They were attacked by around 3,000 rebels. Seven of the troops were killed and about 200 rebels.

In the early hours of the morning, Sunday, May 27, Colonel Campbell marched from Athy to Ballitore. En route he destroyed the mansion of Colonel Keating at Narraghmore. Keating, a liberal, was suspected of complicity with the United Irishmen.

In Ballitore, sometime after 8am on the morning of May 24 the Suffolk Fencibles marched out of the town leaving nine of their men to secure the baggage. Lt Eadie and 23 of the Tyrone Militia marched with their baggage to join their company at Calverstown. an attempted ambush was thwarted and a party of rebels routed in the wood near Narraghmore.

Around 3pm the rebels appeared on the bridge but were turned back by Dr Johnson. A little later some 300 rebels, led by Malachi Delaney on a

Memorial stone at Pike Bridge

HISTORICAL

white horse, occupied the town. Some of the Suffolks left to protect the baggage were killed. Richard, Yeates, a young yeomantry lieutenant, was captured and killed as the rebels fortified Ballitore.

The Quaker community was unharmed. The rebels began to consider their position and Abraham Shackleton mediated with Colonel Campbell in Athy, to allow them to surrender in return for written protections. Campbell lost patience as the rebels delayed and marched his troops out of Athy around midnight on Saturday, May 26.

Around 3pm on Sunday, May 27, intelligence reached the town that the troops were approaching and the rebels fled. The retributions of the soldiers was severe. Suspects were shot and hanged, even Dr Johnson. Having made an example of the town the troops returned to Athy.

Below: Erected on the 200th anniversary of the Rebellion

HISTORICAL

Memorial to all those involved in the Rebellion of 1798, Narraghmore.

Blessed Well at Rathside - Mullaghmast

By John Duffy

Local legend tells that when St Patrick was on his travels towards Glassealy some of his enemies dug a pit in which to trap him. They placed a wild boar in the pit and covered it with twigs and brambles. The plan was that when St Patrick fell into the pit the boar would kill him.

But Patrick was warned of what was in store for him by an old woman. In turn he said he would turn the spot into a well and would bless it and that the water from the well would cure all ailments of the eyes. Many people travelled to the well on pilgrimage down through the years, including Eamon de Valera.

St. John's Well - Davidstown

By Denis Hughes

St. John's Well is situated at Davidstown beside the Calverstown - Narraghmore road. This well is renowned for cures relating to head, eye and throat ailments. Some years ago this well was renovated with the help of Denis, Jimmy and Pat Hughes and Willie and Brendan Kelly. Christy O'Brien, a local carpenter, made a new entrance gate.

While working on the site the workers found medals and old coins, including a large Daniel O' Connell medallion. Paddy Kelly, a local man, informed them that his aunt worked as a housekeeper for O' Connell and it is possible that she may have placed the medallion there. Nearby are the ruins of Davidstown Church and graveyard.

ST. PATRICK'S WELL - GLASSEALY

By John Donovan

On his travels around Ireland St Patrick blessed many wells, including the one at Glassealy.

For many years St. Patrick's Day was celebrated with a parade from Conlon's shop to this well. Several bands took part over the years. A football match was usually held afterwards. These celebrations continued until 1972.

In 1984 a group of local people decided to renovate the well. Their first task was to fence the area. A bridge was then built across the stream to provide access. The well is sunk in a natural rock basin, beneath an old ash tree.

A statue of St. Patrick, sculpted by the late Dick Joynt who lived for a time in Fontstown and who died recently in Co. Wexford, overlooks the well. The whole area is tastefully landscaped and well maintained. Pilgrims visit the well all year round, seeking cures for themselves and friends.

On St. Patrick's Day each year an ecumenical service is held. Locals say water taken from the well will not boil, and attempting to do so will bring bad luck!

The following poem was composed by Tom Plewman. In the second verse, the Patrick to which Uncle Tom refers is the figure of St. Patrick which stands over the well at Glassealy, sculpted by the late Dick Joynt.

St. Patrick's Well, Glassealy.

Your St Patrick is a holy man,
With churches and cathedrals,
Catholic and Protestant;
Your St Patrick is a learned man
With colleges and schools,
Green and red:
Your St Patrick is a healing man
With hospitals and homes
For sick and dying:
Your St Patrick is a pilgrim
Claiming his own Purgatory
May God and Mary and St Patrick be with you

My Patrick is a gentle man
Scarcely four foot tall,
Carved in stone, flat faced,
In simple Celtic style;
He stands alone.
His church is but a few square yards
Of grass and rock and shrubs,
With healing water from the well
Offering peace to all without
May God and Mary be with him.

St. Patrick's Well Glassealy is really a little gem and well worth a visit.

St. Laurence's School Band at St Patrick's Well

HOLY WELLS

The Drummer's Well - Lipstown

Reasearched by Willie Kelly (R.I.P)

The Drummer's Well, Lipstown, is situated 300 yards west from the Pike Bridge. Situated by the side of the road near Lipstown House and in disuse for a long time its history is not well known. The late Willie Kelly, Inchaquire, a local historian of note, researched the history of the well. It concerns the heroism of a 14-year-old boy who sacrificed his life in the cause of Irish Freedom.

He was the only child of an Englishman and an Irishwoman and the family lived in England. He was scarcely more than an infant when his father, a sailor, was drowned at sea. As he grew up he listened avidly to his mother as she told him of the trials and suffering of the people of her native land under English rule.

She had been actively engaged in the Irish struggle in the West of Ireland before her marriage, but had to flee the country to escape arrest and punishment. He heard from her of the methods used by the United Irishmen to send messages to each other. One such method was the beating of a drum which could be heard over the countryside for miles around. At the boy's insistence she brought him a toy drum. When he was 11-years-old she taught him the drumbeat signals she herself had given during active service in Ireland, but she did so only after pledging him to secrecy.

Two years later, in 1797, the young boy was drafted into the English army, where he was trained as a drummer. The following year the regiment to which he was attached was sent to Ireland.

In the 1798 rebellion he was with a company engaged in battle around Lipstown. Greatly outnumbered, the United Irishmen were preparing to retreat, when the boy learned the English soldiers were running out of ammunition. Thereupon he beat out the message on his drum. The message received, the United Irishmen attacked fiercely and routed the soldiers.

However, the captain in charge of the company was familiar with the drumbeat signals and interpreted the information. He shot the boy and the body was thrown in the well. The United Irishmen learned the boy's name and home address from documents they found on the body. They did not disclose the information for fear it would be published in the English newspapers and focus attention on the boy's mother. Today, the boy's name is unknown in the district but his memory is enshrined in the name "Drummer's Well".

There is a small stone erected there with an
inscription that reads as follows:

"Drummerswell
Drummer boy killed here at the battle of
the Pikebridge in 1798."

RELIGION

Ballymount Chapel

By John Duffy

Ballymount Chapel, a familiar landmark on the Dublin to Carlow Road, was built in the years 1876-1878 by Archdeacon Brady. The patron is St Joseph. The local landlord family of Carroll gave the ground for the chapel, school and teacher's residence, for the sum of £40 which did not have to be repaid at that time. When the old school was sold some years ago this £40 was to be repaid. When contacted Colonel Mitchell, who was then resident in the Carroll's former home, declined the money and said to go ahead and sell the school building.

The Bagnalls, a local family noted as very good stonemasons, built the main structure. An elderly lady, Maggie Dwyer, told me she remembered the porches being added some years later. The bell was donated by Farmer Doyle, who lived near Calverstown in the house now owned by Denis Hughes. The stained glass windows at the back of the altar were donated by King and Queen Doyle who lived in the farm owned up to a few years ago by John Dunne. The strange titles were to help distinguish them in their neighbours' minds as they lived quite close to one another. The farmer was recognized as the best farmer in the parish.

Seamus Byrne, of Calverstown Little, has two old statues which are in his family's possession for many years. He was told many times that they were from Ballymount Chapel and were moved when a new set was donated. Jim O'Connor of Calverstown is said to have painted the statues in 1918 when the flu was rampant and he is reputed to have drunk a bottle of whiskey during the work. The doctor in Calverstown at that time was Tom O'Higgins, father of the future presidential candidate and later Chief Justice. His prescription for the flu was a bottle of whiskey and bed; he never lost a patient!

In 1946 the old wooden altar was removed and the present marble altar was fitted. The Bermingham family of Bullhill donated this altar. A tradesman from Earleys of Dublin erected it and Michael Humphries assisted him. As a child attending the nearby school I remember we went in each day to watch the work in progress and wondered where each piece laid out on the floor would eventually be placed. When nearly all the pieces were assembled the big job was to move in the statue of the reclining Jesus being placed in the tomb. Some help from Pat Keatley's men was required and the signal when all was ready was to ring the bell. This was about 2.30pm in the day. Pat Keatley, Martin Heydon, Mick Rourke, Mick Conlon and some of the school chaps turned up to do the job. The big fear was that a finger of hand would be broken off the statue. The altar table was also quite heavy

RELIGION

and required lots of strength to put it in place.

The chapel was freshly plastered on the outside about 1960. The contractor was Carberry from Athy. The Carroll brothers from Dublin, brothers of a former Lord Mayor of Dublin, carried out the work. Also working on this job was Joe Halloran, Paddy O'Connor, Paddy Ward and John Duffy. Some years later the interior was dry-lined and plastered, the contractor this time was Brendan McLoughlin. Peter McEnroe and his team did the plastering and stippling. Fr Jim Kelly was in the parish during the work on the exterior while Fr O'Neill was here when the interior work was carried out. At this time some new seats were fitted, made by Pat Leigh and his men and parishioners donated new confessional boxes.

Many other items around the chapel including holy water fonts, windows and the name plaque were also donated. Paddy Kelly and his sister Bridget left quite an amount of money to Ballymount chapel and this money has been used to carry out many improvements over the years. Fr Mark Curtis was parish priest in Crookstown during the years 1960 to 1965. He had a great love of Ballymount and himself and Ned Ball could be regularly spotted working in the grounds. He was a renowned rose grower who won so many prizes at the RDS that they made him a competition judge. He celebrated daily Mass at Ballymount until failing health prevented him from continuing this practice. He also donated a statue of the Virgin Mary to the chapel. Seamus Byrne brought this statue from Crookstown on a buck rake and tractor. Fr Curtis paid for the statue himself and the original plan was to site it in a grotto to the side of the church but this did not find favour with the church authorities in Dublin. An old quarry to the back of the chapel was the site that was eventually chosen. A small team of dedicated workers prepared the site and the statue was put in place. Fr Curtis retired through ill health and nothing more was done for about six years.

A new curate, Fr Kiely, arrived in Crookstown and he asked that the project be completed. Some of the original workers started back working to a plan drawn by Jim O'Connor. The Behan family of Calverstown was also very involved and gave a lot of support. Money was collected to purchase concrete and shrubs. More than enough was collected and the excess went to parochial funds. Eddie Behan maintained the grotto for many years until the time of his death. Mass is celebrated at the grotto each year on August 15.

My sincere thanks to Willie Byrne, Seamus Byrne and Denis Hughes who provided much valuable information for this piece.

The building of the Grotto at St. Joseph's

RELIGION

Cardinal Cullen

By Kathleen Livingston

Paul Cullen was born on April 29, 1803, at Prospect and received his first education at the Quaker school in Ballitore. At the age of 13 he went to Carlow College and later at 17-years-of-age he travelled to Rome to train as a priest. He was ordained in 1829 and became Rector of the Irish College in Rome. In 1850 Paul Cullen returned to Ireland to take up an appointment as Archbishop of Armagh. He was appointed Apostolic Delegate of the Pope and his first task was to convene a national synod in Thurles.

In 1852 he became the new Archbishop of Dublin and immediately set about upgrading the quality of the church.

Countless churches, schools, hospitals and asylums were built. He established the Catholic University of Ireland, now UCD, and his own seminary, Holy Cross College in Clonliffe. In 1866 he became the first Irishman to be promoted to the rank of Cardinal.

His ancestors hail from Cullenstown, in the parish of Bannow in Wexford. Many of his family entered religious life over the years, including Miss Maher from Kilrush who founded the Convent of Mercy in Athy.

Parochial records show that Cardinal Cullen administered the sacrament of Confirmation to 197 children at Crookstown on August 7, 1854. Cardinal Cullen died at his residence in Eccles Street, Dublin on October 24, 1878 and, at his own request, was buried beneath the High Altar of the Chapel of Holy Cross College, Clonliffe.

In his memory there is a stained glass window in the Church of St Mary and St Laurence, Crookstown.

Parish Priests of Narraghmore Parish.

By John Duffy

The oldest headstones in Crookstown graveyard are those placed along by the wall next to the present St. Lawrence's national school. The headstones were originally in the graveyard that was around the old Parish church (Parish hall). This building later became the boys and girls national school. The building was used as a parish hall and known as the little theatre. The old church closed in 1864 and the old head-stones that were around the church were moved to the present grave yard.

Among the head stones moved were Revered Michael Mernagh and it is possible to read the inscriptions dating from 1731. The recording on the headstone of Revered Michael Mernagh October 12, 1796 is as follows:

"To the memory of the Revered Michael Mernagh thirty four years Parish Priest of Narraghmore pious and unwearied labourer in the Lords vinery and who on the twelfth of October 1796 close in the sixty fifth year of this age a life worn out with apostociacal labour by a death precious in sight of our Lord's religion.

"Weeping for his faithful minister on the twenty second of November 1796 with grateful hand erected this monument. He admonished the rich, to the orphans he was a father, of all ranks of man he deserved well taking himself all to all that he might gain them all to Jesus Christ."

The parochial records go back for more than two hundred and seventy five years.

The following is a list of the pastors:

1728 Very Rev. John Lynch
1762 Very Rev. Michael Mernagh
1803 Very Rev. Michael Cullen
1827 Very Rev. Martin Kelly
1852 Very Rev. Michael Toole
1853 Very Rev. Eugene Clarke
1866 Very Rev. Jeremiah Clarke
1871 Very Rev. Michael Brady
1892 Very Rev. Thomas Carbury
1899 Very Rev. Patrick Warren
1924 Very Rev. Peter Earley
1925 Very Rev. Lawrence Stafford
1942 Very Rev. Malachy Clarke
1948 Very Rev. John O'Doherty
1949-58 Very Rev. Joseph Young
1958-60 Rev. Fr. Gleeson
1960-65 Rev. Fr Mark Curtis
1965-66 Rev. Fr Cosgrave
1966-69 Rev.Fr Moyihan
1970-81 Rev.Fr James Brophy
1981-98 Rev.Fr. Henry O'Connor
1998 to date Rev. Fr.Dempsey.

The parish priests buried in Crookstown graveyard.

- ❖ Fr Joseph Stafford Parish Priest
  1925-1943, Died the 17th May 1943
- ❖ Father John O'Dohery
  1948-1949, Died the 26th May 1949
- ❖ Fr Glesson
  1986-1960, Died 9th October 1960
- ❖ Fr. Moynihan,
  late parish priest of Valleymount and Meath Street and Narraghmore 1898-1969
- ❖ Fr Brophy,
  Died 3rd January 1981
- ❖ Fr Henry O'Connor,
  Died 17th April 1998

Fr. Joseph Young PP with Bishop Dunne. Confirmation 1958.

RELIGION

Fr. Jim Kelly with Tommy Walsh, Confirmation 1958

RELIGION

*Fr. Jim Kelly with Mary, Tom and Pat Gorman,
Confirmation 1958*

The Church of the Holy Saviour, Narraghmore

By Philip Hendy

The Church of the Holy Saviour - Narraghmore

The church and burial ground of Narraghmore is situated in the parish of Narraghmore and in the townland of Narragmore Demesne, part of the Barony of Narrag and Rheban East. It is located a little south of the village of the same name, on the summit of a north south ridge, east of the road between Athy and Kilcullen. The Church of Ireland owns the site and the church and graveyard are still in use. It is a recorded site in the Sites and Monuments Record. (#SMR VOKD:W1)

Tradition states that St Patrick founded a church at Narraghmore in the 5th century. A low, grass covered, wall base, aligned north-south, is said to have belonged to an earlier church which was destroyed by Cromwell. A granite water font, now in the burial ground, may have come from this earlier church.

The foundation stone of the present building was laid by Agnes Augusta Dickenson, wife of the Rector, Charles John Dickenson B.A., on Wednesday, August 27,1862. It was opened for Divine service on Friday July 17, 1863 at 12 noon. The total cost of the building was £400 which was contributed by the Ecclesiastical Commissioners for Ireland.

RELIGION

The chancel is the only portion of the old church, which remains and was built by the Rev J Bonham of Ballintaggart in the year 1849. The east windows and sidelights are memorials to some members of this family and are filled with stained glass ornamented with handsome and appropriate devices. The nave windows of both sides, built in the pointed Gothic style of architecture, are glazed with green rolled Cathedral glass, shedding a "dim" religious light on the substantial stained and varnished principals and cornices of the framed roof. On the floor, which is composed of Staffordshire tiles, each 4"x 4"tile of varied colours is set in a diamond shape with studied regularity.

The pulpit and prayer desk are both stained and varnished open woodwork. The buttresses, doorways, porches and windows are formed of Kilkenny granite, the interior quoins being caen stone. The mason work of the walls is greenish flagstone, abounding in the area, similar to the style adapted in building the Corn Exchange in Athy.

The size of the entire structure is 76'x 20'. The western gable is surmounted by an elegantly proportioned spire, supported by a massive buttress, the entire being nearly 60' high. At the base of the spire there is a gargoyle, a medieval Griffins head, ornamented with dog's ears with open mouth and staring eyes. The roof has Welsh slates on it with an ornamental ridge crest. A gilded weathercock and cross surmount the bell spire.

The architect was RJ Withers, of Doughty St, London, and the builder was FH Carroll of Dublin. There were clergy at the official opening and Mrs Dickenson, the rector's wife presided at the harmonium. There were 154 people present and the collection amounted to £20.

Rev. Kennerely with Bishop Walsh at an ecumenical service in Narraghmore.

below: the beautiful stained glass windows are well worth a look.

The Mission

By John Duffy

When Father Dempsey announced that we were to have a Parish Mission in October it set me thinking about those missions we had years ago. Those times it was announced at Mass that we were to have a mission in two weeks time and that it would be given by a member of the Redemptorist Order.

The missioner usually arrived and said Sunday morning Mass. This was the signing up time. We would be looking and wondering what he was going to be like and he would be doing the same with us. The first thing I noticed was his strong voice in these pre microphones days. Usually it was a fairly mild sermon to begin with. He would talk of the times of the ceremonies and that he expected everyone to attend as it was only for a week, and it might be the last chance for some of us to save our souls.

Fr. Vincent Dempsey in Fatima 2003

Sunday night he was quiet enough but still the view among us was that he could yet be wicked. Monday night was calm enough, but still he stressed that we were all in need of change from those bad habits that had come over us.

Tuesday night was usually about "keeping company" and the terrible dangers of mortal sin. Wednesday and Thursday nights were devoted to the other big dangers, stealing your neighbour's property or character or maybe his wife, intemperance or getting drunk and neglecting your wife and children. He would shout and strut around the altar and we all felt we were very much in need of God's mercy or the devil had a full harvest in Ballymount alone.

The next big question on our minds was what would he be like in confession? A few old ladies, who would have nothing serious to tell, did not give us much to go on. It was only when the hard men went in and were not detained very long, that the watchers began to gain a bit of courage, and in truth his bark was worse than his bite.

The other attraction that arrived with the mission was a wooden frame canvas shop in which all the holy pictures, key rings, scapulars, holy water fonts, St. Christopher's medals, prayer books, crucifixes, rosary beads, plus the pouches to carry them in were available for sale. The woman who owned this stall came from Dublin and stayed in some of the local houses. When not busy in the stall she made rosary beads and could cut and bend the fine wire and tread on the beads while still talking to her customers. All these objects were blessed at the closing of the mission.

The parish committee had lots of candles on sale for the ceremony for the renewal of baptismal vows. The chapel was packed with people and you had to be early to get a seat. The choir in full voice gave the service a great atmosphere with the missioner telling us all how good we were. We could nearly see the halos on our heads! He always administered the pledge and it was up to yourself to take it or not. The final hymn was always Faith of our Fathers and everyone came out in the best of form.

The general feeling was that it was a week well spent and an added bonus was that as we had been getting up early in the morning to attend the mission we got more work done as well as looking after our souls.

We always said we would to at least one night to Crookstown the following week, but when the time came we were nearly back in our old ways and failed to go. Billy Martin of Ballitore provided the taxi service to bring the missioner back and forward to Crookstown. Billy had a blue Ford car that was spotless, likewise Billy himself, very much the professional driver.

The Opening of Crookstown Chapel

By John Duffy

The Altar - Crookstown Church

St Patrick came to Ireland in the year 432 and set about converting the natives to Christianity. On his travels around Ireland he visited Killeen Cormac which was a Druidic settlement at the time. The chief family was called Dubtaig, the English translation of which means Duffy, who were not related to us as far as I know.

St. Patrick also visited Glassealy and Mullaghmast where he blessed wells. His mission in this parish must have been very successful as chapels were built in Usk, Kyle, Moyleabbey, Davistown, Glassealy and Narraghmore. Some of these chapels were probably very simply constructed as very little trace of them has survived.

Davidstown has the finest ruins. Legend has it that this building was never completed with a roof but some believe that Davidstown was completed and used as a chapel until the Reformation, after which the roof fell in through neglect. The local Protestants then roofed it to use as a church but the day it was finished wind came and blew the roof off it again. When Cromwell was here in 1649 his cannon levelled the chapel in Narraghmore.

RELIGION

On a hill at Crookstown, in view of the present chapel, there was a Mass rock and this is where they celebrated the divine mysteries. That hill is still known as Crookanavin, the hill of the Mass. I refer to these buildings as chapels. Up until a few years ago a chapel was a place of worship for Roman Catholics and a church was for Protestant worship. Not later than 1720 a plot of ground was procured at Crookstown and a chapel was built. This building was first roofed with thatch and sometime later was re-roofed and slated.

During the rebellion of 1798 a battle was fought at the Pike Bridge. Malachy Delaney, a native of Calverstown, led the insurgents. A Protestant family, the Hendys of Mullamoy, sheltered him and eventually he made his escape to America.

Some 20 years later he returned to Ireland and, on disembarking at Cobh, learned that all his family had died. On his way back to Kildare the coach overturned and Delaney's hip was broken. As he was dying he made his will giving what money he had to the priest in Crookstown to have seats for the chapel made. At that time the people brought bundles of straw and rushes to kneel on, the same as in Nurney and all the chapels around.

The seats were made by a Ballitore man and were of a plain construction, with a single rail along the back. When times got better these seats went to Ballymount, and were later sold to Father Ramsbottom in Suncroft. This information about the seats was obtained from Father Swaine's book on 1798 in County Kildare.

That first chapel at Crookstown was of Cruciform shape and served this parish as a chapel for close on 40 years. Cardinal Cullen administered Confirmation to 197 children on August 7, 1854. This old chapel was later turned into a boys' and girls' school. All that now remains of it is the Little Theatre.

Building work on the present parish chapel started on May 3, 1860 and was completed on September 29, 1867. Although the building was not completed until 1867, the first Mass was offered in it in 1864. The bell in the tower was rung for the first time on Hallow's Eve, 1867. The builders took the precaution of putting a piece of leather on the striker in case the vibrations of the bell would damage the tower. The cost of the building was £1,500, a lot of money 140 years ago, and it must have taken a huge effort to complete.

It is built in the Celtic-Romanesque style. It has a graceful doorway of recessed arches in granite that are reminiscent of the very beautiful doorway of the ancient Cathedral of Clonfert. The granite pillars are from Ballyknockan quarries, and it is believed they arrived, one at a time, on a special type of four-wheel wagon, drawn by two horses.

Among the many improvements to the chapel since its erection are the four beautiful, stained glass windows, one of which contains a good portrait of Cardinal Cullen. These windows cost

£500 when erected during Fr. Carberry's pastorship 1892-1899. The marble communion rails, with a brass gate in the centre, a replica of the one in Armagh Cathedral, were erected in 1905. The memorial pulpit to the Reverend A Clarke, Archdeacon Brady and Father Thomas Carberry, was erected a year later in 1906. The tiling in the front of the altar rails was laid in 1925 at a cost of £360.

The removal of the altar rails, brass gates and pulpit under the Second Vatican Council did not please some people in this parish, myself included. The present lectern was constructed from portions of the pulpit, as was the one in Ballymount. Mc Carthy was the architect over the building of this chapel and over a period of 30 years he built over 60 chapels in the diocese, including Kilcullen and Roundwood, finishing up with Clonliffe College.

As the present major renovation programme draws to a close we look back in admiration at our ancestors and the effort it took 140 years ago to build this chapel, little more than 10 years after the famine of 1847. We pray for them and thank them. Our hope is that when the next major renovations are carried out in 100 or 150 years that the people living in the Parish of Narraghmore will think of us and say a prayer for us.

In the meantime all concerned with this magnificent job of restoration can take pride in a huge task successfully undertaken and completed. Crookstown chapel now looks better than ever. Father Dempsey must be mentioned for special thanks, in the way he kept his team motivated and focused. To everyone concerned thanks very much for a job well done.

Crookstown Church

BALLITORE - A QUAKER VILLAGE

By Mary Malone

Early postcard of Ballitore

The Religious Society of Friends, or Quakers, is a Christian group that originated in Yorkshire, England in 1650. Established by George Fox, a gentleman who objected to the rituals and formality of organised religion, the Quakers quickly increased in numbers and the first Quaker who arrived in Ireland in 1653 was William Edmundson. He is buried in Rosenallis, Co. Laois. William Penn came to Cork in 1666 to manage his father's estates. He moved to America sometime afterwards where he founded the state of Pennsylvania.

The first Quakers to arrive in Ballitore were Abel Strettel and John Barcroft and they built Ballitore House sometime after 1685. The Retreat (in the grounds of the present Glanbia factory), Griesebank House, Ballitore Mill (now in ruins) and Fullers Court, were other Quaker houses built over the next few years. The Meeting House was built in 1708 and Griesemount House in 1816.

Abraham Shackleton started the Quakers Boys' Boarding School in Ballitore in 1726. The school was international as well as inter-denominational and attracted students from as far away as Jamaica and Norway. Edmund Burke, Napper Tandy and a local man, Paul Cullen, who later became Archbishop of Dublin and Ireland's first Cardinal, all received their early education there. William Leadbeater, who was of French Huguenot decent, also went to school in Ballitore. He later attended Trinity College Dublin, where he qualified in law. He converted to Quakerism, gave up his legal practice in Dublin and came back to live in Ballitore where he took up farming. He married Mary Shackleton, daughter of Richard and Elizabeth, and granddaughter of Abraham, who founded the Quaker school, in 1791 and lived in the present Mary Leadbeater House. Mary was the first postmistress in Ballitore but was also well known for her writings which included The Annals of Ballitore, Cottage Biographies, and Booklets for Quaker Children. They had three daughters. Mary died in 1826 and William in 1827 and both are buried in the Quaker Graveyard, just opposite the garda station.

The Bewley family had strong associations with Ballitore. Living in the area for a short while around 1801, they would have opened the tannery back then. The Goodbody boys would have attended school in Ballitore and later lived in Clara, where the family had a well-known jute factory. The Pim boys went to school in Ballitore also and went on to distinguish themselves in the family drapery business in George's Street, Dublin for quite some years. These are but a few of the Quaker families who had strong associations with the area.

Old Quaker Meeting House - Ballitore

Today, no Quakers live in the actual village of Ballitore but there are some members of the society living in Moone. They meet each Sunday morning in the Meeting House and welcome people of other religious denominations to join them for their meetings. Quakers believe simplicity, purity and truthfulness to be of paramount importance. The last census tells us Ballitore has a population of approximately 750 people. It is a village proud of its Quaker origins and with a bright future ahead of it.

SOCIAL LIFE

Ballitore ICA

By Lily O'Meara

Ballitore ICA was formed in the Town Hall in Ballitore in 1963 and there are a number of founder members still involved in the branch. In the beginning the meetings were held in the old school where the members had to bring their own fuel for the stove and hope the kettle would boil in time for the tea. Thanks to Mr Sloan, school principal and Fr Brophy PP they were allowed access to the new school for their meetings when it was opened. Oh what comfort!

Over the years the ladies involved have learned crafts and needlework such as embroidery, glove making, basketmaking, decoupage, quilting, both English and Italian, crochet, macramé, glass etching, sougan stools and patchwork. Some of the members discovered they had a flair for painting after taking lessons from a local artist.

From time to time the ICA invites professionals to come and speak with them and they have had talks from solicitors, beauticians, aromatherapists, reflexologists etc.

Since its formation the guild has raised money for the parish, the school, the Irish Kidney Association, the blind, Care of the Elderly, and have catered for special occasions for nearly every organization and event in the parish.

They have an outing ever summer and a night-out at Christmas and they have also enjoyed weekends in Wales and a holiday to Europe where they visited all the EU establishments, had dinner with the MEPs and sat in at a session of the European Parliament.

They are a small in number, but are a happy little group and are always delighted to welcome new members. They meet on the second Tuesday of every month at which they have a guest to give a talk or demonstration.

The ICA still going strong
(*Photo circa 1985*)

SOCIAL LIFE

Ballitore Library

By Mary Malone

Ballitore library and museum were originally housed in the Quaker Meeting House but have recently relocated to the Mary Leadbeater House in the centre of the village.

When I came to Ballitore back in November 1998 the library and museum were in one large room in the Meeting House. I have to admit, coming from working in a much busier library and being with other colleagues all day, it was strange in the beginning to readjust to the quietness of the Meeting House. Gradually I got to know my stock and became familiar with my surroundings and decided to focus on the children to begin with. "Mol an oige agus tiocfaidh siad" as the old saying goes.

The library has become a focal point for the village and is home to a number of active groups. The local children enjoy using the facilities and taking part in the various competitions organised. The library was the birthplace of the active Griese Players drama group for children and it also hosted the meetings of the local Humpty Dumpty mother and toddlers club. There is also an active homework club in operation. We meet once a week and an extra benefit for the children is whenever visitors come in to the museum they are always invited to chat with the children, particularly if they come from abroad. The children often go home with first hand knowledge of countries that might not have been on their current school curriculum. The Fainne Women's Group also used the library for their meetings which has also hosted workshops for creative writing.

The library attracts many visitors from near and far. Some want to know about their ancestors, more want to know about the history of the village, more just like to read the local history books that are available. Each visitor is different and a challenge. I noticed that all who came in and had some snippets of information about some aspect of life in the village were always more than willing to share that information with me. My local history file is now nearly at two volumes.

Thanks to the perseverance and hard work of a group of local people and with the help of FÁS, Kildare County Council and other relevant bodies the Mary Leadbeater House was completely restored by 2001. I was given the brief to relocate the library there and help with the setting up of the museum. This was another big change, as I now would have a two - storied house to look after, as opposed to one huge big room that housed everything. In April last year the library reopened at its new base in the centre of the village. Just before Christmas the internet access room opened with three

SOCIAL LIFE

computers for public use. Both facilities have made an enormous impact on the lives of so many people. One young man who was unemployed has, over the last few months, taught himself so much on he wants to work full time on them now. Another senior citizen is a wizard on them as well and would put many of us to shame with her newfound knowledge.

More and more group tours are coming in and no two days are ever the same. They enjoy the warm atmosphere of the Mary Leadbeater House and if the weather allows them, the pleasure of the Mary Leadbeater Garden as well.

So much has happened in Ballitore through the library in the last four and a half years that it is hard to quantify. All of the successes were ideas brought to me by the local people and through the facilities at my disposal we brought them to fruition.

The people themselves, proud of their local history and heritage have made their local library and museum a place to be proud of.

If you haven't already paid a visit, put it on your agenda as a "must do" for this year. You won't regret it.

The Library and Museum is now located in the Mary Leadbeater House

SOCIAL LIFE

BALLITORE PICTURE HOUSE

Ballitore Picture House opened around 1946 or 1947 and provided many, many hours of entertainment for the people of the area. It was located in an old barn owned by the O'Connor family which was renovated and fitted out as a cinema. Its patrons were drawn from the local area and the same people returned week after week on Sunday and Wednesday nights to enjoy the entertainment.

As the films were usually on two separate reels this meant a break halfway through the show. The younger members of the audience used to enjoy counting down from 10 to one, as the new reel was lined up on the projector.

There were lots of Westerns, comedies and newsreels. Abbot & Costello, Laurel & Hardy and Charlie Chaplin were some of the most popular stars of the day.

Pat O'Connor went around the local area on his motorbike on a Saturday calling on shops with posters to advertise the forthcoming attractions.

Bernard Higgins travelled on the pillion with a roll of posters stuck in his coat, carrying a bucket of paste for pasting the posters on selected trees.

Jimmy Gibbons and Christy Higgins were the main projectionists. Joseph O'Connor, Pat's father, was on the door. As television became more popular the number of patrons decreased and the picture house finally closed in 1965.

Ballitore Village c1963.

Card Playing

by Paddy Doyle

Mary Anne Lawlor and Anne Gorman - card playing friends

Card playing as a pastime goes back a long way in rural Ireland and the parish of Narraghmore and the surrounding areas was no exception. We have all heard stories of great 25 players and the games that were played in houses in every townland and of the arguments that might arise. If the situation looked like getting out of hand the woman of the house would collect up the cards and put them in the fire. But of course someone would get a new pack for the next night and so it continued.

In the early 1950s Fr Jack Whelan, a Dublin man, came to Kilmead as a curate. A very enterprising man, he had a great interest in card playing and also in boxing. It was he who organised the first of many big 25 drives in aid of parochial funds which were held in the Little Theatre, Crookstown, in mid March each year. The event attracted huge crowds each year and continued right up to the mid 1960s. The staging of the event called for a lot of organising and a good deal of hard work. A huge marquee had to be erected, along with several smaller

SOCIAL LIFE

tents, to accommodate the card players and to provide space for catering. A large working committee was involved which helped to make the workload lighter for everyone. Sadly most of that committee has since passed away.

With the advent of television the popularity of organised card playing seemed to wane with very few big games taking place.

During the 1980s the local athletic club revived 25 drives in Crookstown as a means of raising funds. While these games were quite successful they never attracted the crowds that attended some 20 years previously.

In 1988 the athletic club changed from 25 drives to whist drives as a means of raising funds. While very few locals played the game then, a programme of lessons for beginners which started in October 1989 changed all that, with the result that a thriving game of whist has been played in Kelly's function room every Wednesday night for the past 13 years.

Poker too has been a popular game in the parish down through the years, with many people able to recall the names of famous players who, during their lifetime, won and lost fortunes at the game. The game of poker today is probably a little more ordered with poker classics being organised in different places as fundraisers for various causes. But you can rest assured that there are still some high flyers who are prepared to gamble as much, if not more, than the poker players of the past. While card playing generally may never be as widespread or as popular again as it was in the pre television days I think it will survive, especially in rural areas. It would be a great pity indeed if people were to let a great Irish pastime die out.

Left: Mona Mc Donnell playing whist in Narraghmore

SOCIAL LIFE

Just look at the concentration going into this game!

No cameras please!

SOCIAL LIFE

The Copper Beach at Poplar Hall

By John Duffy

My early years are just a dim memory of which very little can I remember. But then, as it is 300 years at least since I was first planted here in Poplar Hall you must excuse my memory failing me. The feel of the warm moist soil around my roots as they got stronger and ever deeper into the ground made me feel happy and contented. As I grew I started to take notice of my surroundings. My sister, planted 30 yards away from me, near a very small yew tree and a very new looking house gave me to think that we were all around the one age.

The family living in the house were named Farmer, husband and wife, plus three small children. The children played tig around us and we were a little afraid of getting damaged. The years passed as the children grew into adults, left home and visited again when on holidays. This went on for years and we trees grew bigger and stronger.

Now a new generation of children made a swing from one of my branches while the others played hide and seek around my big trunk. Occasionally a big coach, drawn by four horses, would come up the drive and pass around by me. This made me very happy. I often heard Mr John farmer talk to Colonel Keating about unrest in the country and they were worried. In May 1798, when I was about 100 years old, all the houses in Narraghmore were burnt and a battle was fought along the bog road about 400 yards from where I stood. Luckily we were not on the edge of the road or we would have met the same fate as the other trees around that were felled and used as barricades to block the road. As I had grown the tallest and could see everything I had to tell the others what was happening. I saw the 14 Redcoats who turned up to help the insurgents being captured and brought to Dunlavin to be shot.

When the famine came around here it was terrible, the lovely drills of potatoes were just getting ready to blossom and overnight were turned to stinking, rotting pulp. Almost overnight the sound of the children laughing and playing stopped and a terrible silence descended on the whole area. The Farmer family was fairly well off and was able to buy small amounts of expensive imported food. Some of the young people around left for America and we never saw them again. At this stage I was my full height and had a lovely copper hue to my foliage and was now about 150 years of age.

The family named Farmer all got old and died and this place was sold to a new family named Murray who let the place go to rack and run and just kept a few stallion horses. This was quite a big business as lots of the local farm-

SOCIAL LIFE

Elizabeth Duffy at Poplar Hall

ers bred horses and sold them to the army, especially when war threatened. The Murray family sold most of the land around the house, leaving just 30 acres. When the Murray family died the place was sold to new people by the name of Duffy. They started doing up the house and after about a year arrived with a family of eight children and mother and father.

These people were teachers and the children played around us, climbed us and made a big change from the Murray family. The children grew into adults and forgot all about us trees, passing in and out with scarcely a glance in our direction.

The first World War was on at this stage and we heard terrible stories of death and destruction. Then the Civil War at home caused a lot of trouble in this family. A few quiet years and then war again in 1939.

At this stage I was feeling the years as I was nearly 250 years old. After another 20 years my sister, also a copper beech, died and was cut down for firewood.

In 1970 John and Bridie Duffy came to live here and very soon had nine children, plus a lot of cats and dogs. One of the dogs even had a litter of pups in my rotting roots.

At Easter time the Easter Bunny always left some eggs under my hollowed, rotting trunk. The children got wise and went looking there first. This made me very happy as the sound of happy children was always my favourite sound.

These last few winters have been very hard on me and on October 20, 2002, at 5.30am I could no longer hold on and hit the ground with a big bang. I heard Noel, who was inside the house, saying "Bugs Bunny is down, she blew out into the field". Out came John and Noel with a lamp to view the corpse. Then the whole house was awake with lights on everywhere. The one thing that I was glad about was that the house had escaped.

Now everyone is amazed at my size and say what a huge tree I was. I was the oldest living thing around for miles and protected the house from storms for hundreds of years.

Now I will keep the house warm for about two years and when gazing into the flames I hope they will think of me. I hear talk of making a small table from some of my wood or a fancy dish, so maybe my life is not over, just yet.

SOCIAL LIFE

How Hickeys of Calverstown got its name

By Joe Hickey

I stand proudly at the cross roads in Calverstown and have done so for hundreds of years. I have had many names over three centuries and am known today as Hickey's and this is the background as to how I got my name.

The early 1920s were dangerous and treacherous times in Ireland. The unified fight for Irish independence ended in January 1922 when the British handed over power to the Provisional Government. This was to be followed by the Civil War when friends, family and neighbours fought one another with both sides convinced of the justness and rights of their cause.

On the one side were the pro-Treaty forces known as the "Free Staters" who supported the new 26-county State set out under the terms of the Treaty negotiated with the British Government and ratified narrowly by the first Dáil by 64 votes to 57.

The anti-Treaty side, led by Eamon De Valera, withdrew from the Dáil and

SOCIAL LIFE

were described in pejorative terms as "the Irregulars". The anti-Treaty side felt that the terms could not be accepted by genuine Republicans as they were completely contrary to the ideals espoused by Tone, Emmet and Pearse, containing as it did the necessity for the Irish Dáil members to swear an oath of allegiance to the King of England, retention of control of certain Ireland ports by the British Government, the payment of land annuities to Britain and the occupation of six of the 32-counties by British forces.

During the Civil War an active member of one side was a fair target for the other side- these were dangerous and treacherous times.

Arthur Griffith was the founder of Sinn Féin, leader of the Treaty negotiating team and a signatory of the Treaty on December 6, 1921. He was appointed President of the Provisional Government after Eamon De Valera withdrew the anti-Treaty side from the first Dáil following the ratification of the Treaty. Griffith was a staunch defender of the Treaty and he died suddenly on August 12, 1922, 10 days before Michael Collins, the other colossus of the pro-Treaty side, was shot by anti-Treaty forces in his native Cork.

The Provisional Government ordered a State funeral for the President and local pro-Treaty forces (Free Staters) throughout the country felt it fitting that all businesses should close as a

SOCIAL LIFE

The wedding of Mick Hickey and Elsie Lee in 1940 with Sheila Kehily, bridesmaid and the late Batty Kelly, Mick Hickey's cousin - best man

mark of respect on the day of Griffith's burial. Individuals were deployed to convince business owners of the significance of the gesture.

It was a sunny afternoon in Calverstown on August 14, 1922. A young man dressed in a long, black leather military style coat entered Calverstown on his motorbike. He was the young 'Free Stater' who had the task of convincing the owners of Patrick Lee's grocery, hardware, drapery and public house in Calverstown, to close the premises on the day of Griffith's funeral.

Patrick Lee was a successful business man who was involved in a number of businesses, a public house in Athy, his business in Calverstown, and with his brother James in Lee's of Ballyshannon, (now Dowling's). He hailed from Suncroft and set up business in Calverstown in the late 1890s and married Anastasia Bermingham from Bull Hill who was many years his junior. They had one child, Elsie, who was born in 1911. Patrick Lee died on January 21, 1921 and was survived by his wife and their nine-year-old daughter. Lee Drive in Calverstown bears his name today.

It was Patrick Lee's widow, Anastasia, who was behind the counter when the young 'Free Stater' entered the front door leading to the grocery and hardware area. He was formidable looking in his long, military style black leather coat and it was obvious at close quarters, that he was armed. He asked to speak with Anastasia.

Anastasia did not suffer fools gladly, nor what she regarded as local vigilantes, belonging to either the pro or anti Treaty sides. She had faced down more formidable opposition than the young 'Free Stater' and told him so.
Extreme Irish nationalists saw World War 1 (1914-1918) as an Imperialist war between superpowers, but more importantly saw it as a golden opportunity to strike a blow for Irish independence. Following the abortive 1916 rebellion in Dublin, 16 of the insurgents were executed, transforming the ambivalent population's sympathies to a more nationalist, republican ideal and galvanizing support for the Irish cause.

In 1919, the War of Independence began in the form of a guerrilla war. The objective was to attack isolated RIC (Royal Irish Constabulary) stations in rural Ireland to drive police and army back into the cities and major towns.

To counteract this strategy and retake the rural areas, in March 1920, the British introduced a force known as the Black n'Tans. They were known as Black n' Tans because of the distinctive colours of their uniforms. 1920 was known as a year of terror and mayhem. The Black n'Tans were recruited as an auxiliary police force from weary, unemployed, shell-shocked soldiers who had returned from service in the 1914-1918 war. The popular myth was that they were the sweepings of English prisons and proved to be an undisciplined, brutal, callous cabal of renegades who rained terror, murder, and mayhem on those unfortunate enough to cross their path.

In order to instill fear in the hearts of the Irish people the Black n' Tans were always open to suitable opportunities to demonstrate their power and the futility of Irish resistance.

In January 1921 Patrick Lee was away from Calverstown on business, his shop was surrounded by the Black n' Tans and the occupants, Anastasia Lee and her nine-year-old daughter Elsie, were ordered to leave. The premises were to be burnt down because the Black n' Tans felt that the public house was being used by individuals engaged in the Irish resistance.

Anastasia Lee was made of sterner stuff and would not vacate the premises. The siege lasted only one hour. It is believed that the premises were not torched because the shop contents, which the Black n' Tans wished to loot, would have been destroyed, the age of young Elsie Lee and the intervention of a local clergyman.

If Anastasia Lee was prepared to face down the Black n' Tans she was not going to allow the young 'Free Stater' vigilante to dictate to her when he called on August 14, 1922.

The young 'Free Stater' had also crossed swords with the Black n'Tans. He lived in Narraghmore and had been actively involved in the resistance to British occupation. He was born in 1897 and was 23 years of age when the Black n'Tans arrived. Within his family home was a secret compartment which was used by the young 'Free Stater' and his comrades. Many times they occupied the Moat of Ardscull which is on high ground overlooking the approach roads, north of Athy on the main Athy-Dublin road. It enabled them to attack, at will, the Black n'Tan forces, pin them down and inflict as much damage, death and injury as possible, followed by a clean, quick getaway. But the young 'Free Stater's' luck ran out.

The Irish cause, down the centuries, has always been dogged by informers. On a bitterly cold winter's day in 1920, after a tip-off, the Black n'Tans surrounded his family home, entered it and walked directly to the secret compartment. Both he and a colleague were beaten and transported to the Curragh for what they thought was incarceration. On the edge of the Curragh they were thrown to the ground, whipped, kicked and pum-

SOCIAL LIFE

meled to unconsciousness, stripped and thrown into a pond and left for dead. Fortunately through the help of local sympathisers, they were rescued, rested and returned to Narraghmore.

On that day in August 1922 it was a stand-off between Anastasia Lee and the young 'Free Stater' to be broken only by the interjection of Anastasia's brother, Tom Bermingham from Bull Hill (where Tom Hickey now resides, half way between Narraghmore and Calverstown). He was helping his widowed sister to run the business. He was aware of the young 'Free Stater's' credentials and was also convinced that Griffith was a patriot, not because of his pro-Treaty allegiances but because of his personal sacrifices for Ireland's freedom, along with Michael Collins just as on the anti-treaty side were the patriot figures of Erskine Childers, Cathal Brugha and Eamon de Valera.

Tom Bermingham succeeded in convincing his sister but not before Anastasia made it clear that her objections were not political but personal- she would not take orders from pro or anti-Treaty vigilantes.

Anastasia Lee survived her husband by 53 years. She never remarried and wore black every day until her death in 1973.

So where did the name 'Hickey's of Calverstown' come from? Elsie Lee, who was nine years of age when the Black n'Tans laid siege to her home grew up to be a beautiful young lady and was much sought after by suitors, not just for her beauty and personality but in addition, by the more shallow suitors, because of her not inconsiderable material assets which she inherited from her father.

Her mother, Anastasia, was neither retiring nor reserved about expressing her opinions and guidance on the relative merits of her suitors but she was ill-prepared for her daughter's choice. The man who was to win her hand was the young 'Free Stater' who strode into her home on that sunny afternoon on August 14, 1922 with the mission of closing the premises for the day of Arthur Griffith's funeral. He was Michael (Mick) Hickey from Narraghmore, (from the post office and shop on the crossroads in Narraghmore). In 1975, following substantial renovations, the name of Patrick Lee was removed from the premises and replaced by Hickey's.

While Anastasia Lee may have forgiven Mick Hickey for his exploits on that fateful day in 1922, she never forgot the effrontery exhibited by the young 'Free Stater'. Mick and Elsie had one daughter and five sons.

The premises passed out of the ownership of the Hickey family in 2001 but it still bears the Hickey name today.

SOCIAL LIFE

Patrick Lee and Anastasia Bermingham

SOCIAL LIFE

Industry in the Parish

By Paddy Doyle

SMALL villages in rural Ireland that could claim to have a thriving industry in the early 20th century were few and far between. Not so Ballitore which had a long established tannery yard, producing first-class leather under the management of the Cullen family. The business closed in the early 1940s, leaving the village without an industry for the first time in many generations. About 1955 the Barrowvale Co-Op creamery, based in Goresbridge, County Kilkenny, had extended its collection area into west Wicklow and south Kildare. Milk production for sale was something completely new for small and medium sized farmers in the area, but the need for a regular monthly income encouraged many to adapt to this new style of farming.

The Barrowvale collection area continued to grow, extending as far north as the County Dublin border by 1960. It was then that the co-op saw the need to establish a branch creamery somewhere in this area. Ballitore was the favoured location and building work

AT OFFICIAL OF BARROWVALE CREAMERY, BALLITORE JUNE 1964
Front Row (L to R): J. Logan, N. Leigh, W.M. Miley, W.M. Fennelly (Manager), W. Stanley, D. Nolan
Back Row: P. Byrne, B. Lennon, P. Kelly, J. O'Mara, M. Lawler, M. McGee, P. Doyle, M. Kirwan, J. Dallon

SOCIAL LIFE

Barrow Vale Creamery 1964

began straight away on a site purchased from Mr Michael Kirwan. The branch creamery commenced operations in 1962 and the official opening was performed by the then Minister for Agriculture, Mr Paddy Smith, on Monday, June 8, 1964.

Throughput of milk continued to grow each year, but the back-up service to suppliers in the line of feedstuffs, hardware etc. seemed to lag behind, until the arrival of Jim Fitzharris, an enterprising young County Carlow man, as manager in 1971.

The erection of a large store, containing a shop and office, was the first sign of the expansion that was soon to follow. Having carried out a survey of the grain growing potential of the catchment area around Ballitore the manager persuaded the co-op that a grain intake, with drying facilities, would be a good investment and so the first grain silos were erected in the summer of 1975, in preparation for the harvest to follow.

The manager's judgement was certainly vindicated, with the volume of grain increasing year by year through the '70s and '80s. Through these years, under the expert management of Jim Fitzharris, the volume of business grew dramatically with huge amounts of feedstuff, fertilizers, chemicals, seed grain and general hardware being collected by farmers or delivered to their yards.

The early '70s was indeed a time of great change in the creamery milk business, when 30 societies, including Barrowvale, amalgamated to form Avonmore Creameries Ltd. This led to the introduction of bulk collection and the demise of the milk churn, which

SOCIAL LIFE

had been a symbol of the business for generations. Up until now creamery milk production had been, by tradition, a seasonal operation with the bulk of the milk produced during the grazing season. This was not very economical, so farmers in the Ballitore area were encouraged to produce winter milk for liquid consumption. There was a great response and soon new buildings were erected and new equipment installed to cater for the processing system which was to change the face of Ballitore creamery beyond recognition.

Further expansion took place following the amalgamation of Avonmore and Waterford Co-Op, which also included Dublin Dairies. Huge volumes of milk were now being processed in Ballitore for distribution all over Leinster and beyond. The company, in the meantime, changed its name to Glanbia and is now one of the major players in the milk business in Ireland. Ballitore milk processing plant, combined with its grain intake and argi-business section is the biggest employer in the area with well in excess of 100 people on its payroll, a far cry from 1962 when the staff consisted of a manager and three employees.

The Glanbia complex, as it stands today, is a monument to the wisdom and foresight of the members of the Barrowvale Co-Op who built that small branch creamery in Ballitore and to the commitment, dedication and hard work of the managers and the numerous staff members, who over the past 40 years, have given their all in the interest of a great local industry.

Official opening ceremony 1964

Mayo exodus to Kildare

by Mary Mc Namee

The Gorman Family 1993

St Patrick's Eve, March 16, 1956 was the day that seven families from the Swinford area of County Mayo bade farewell to friends and relations in their native county and travelled to County Kildare to put down their roots in Blackhall, Calverstown, Kilcullen. Although this was their postal address Narraghmore was to be their new parish.

The transplantation from Mayo to Kildare took place as a result of a policy adopted by the Irish Land Commission (1881-1980). This policy was one of migration. The Land Commission implemented this policy during the 1930s, '40s and '50s right up to the '60s to redress the imbalance of ownership of land in rural Ireland. The struggling small farmers, living on small holdings west of the Shannon, supplemented their income by taking the boat to England for nine months of the year, while the women remained at home looking after the small farms and rearing their families and in some cases looking after their elderly parents.

SOCIAL LIFE

In the midlands there were large tracts of land in the ownership of gentlemen farmers and absentee landlords. This land was under utilised. It was as a result of this policy that the Irish Land Commission acquired the Ashe Estate in Blackhall in the early 1950s.

The estate was divided into seven holdings, ranging in size from 33 to 40 acres, with some plots of approx 10-15 acres being offered to former employees of the estate. A new road was built, seven new houses and out offices were constructed and hedges were planted to subdivide the large pasture fields.

Meanwhile, back in Mayo, a number of owners of small holdings had applied to the Land Commission to be considered for a new farm in the midlands.

Around October/November 1955, a Land Commission official informed five families in the townland of Woods and one each in the neighbouring townlands of Castleroyan and Kinaffe that there were seven farms about to be distributed in County Kildare. A date was set for inspection. The men travelled back from England, meeting their wives in the town of Kilcullen, before going on to inspect the holdings in Blackhall. They returned to Mayo together, spending the next few days considering the options that would change the course of their lives forever.

It was not the first time some of the families had looked at farms in the midlands, and had turned down the offer, but it was the first time a whole community had received an offer to live in close proximity to each other.

The late Delia & John Byrne on a day out 1980

SOCIAL LIFE

They all decided to make the move to Kildare. The date of departure was set for March 16, 1956.

There were mixed feelings. Children looked forward to a life where Daddy didn't have to be away from home so much. Fathers and mothers thought long and hard about the decision. Making a living on 35 acres was not going to be easy. The fear of migrating to a strange part of the country was daunting for the women, but, on balance, they felt they could offer their children a brighter future by accepting the offer. Grandparents weren't happy about the move. The upheaval of leaving family and friends behind was disturbing in old age.

The day of departure arrived. The village of Woods was in mourning. Those going away were now full of enthusiasm, optimism and anticipation. For those left behind it was the death of a village. There were 14 houses in Woods in 1956. Five of the doors would now be closed. 30 people were leaving, men and women, grandparents, lively, smiling children. I was one of those children.

Tears were shed by those left behind and a few by those leaving. In the past 49 years only one family was raised in the village of Woods. Two of the seven families that travelled to Kildare came from two neighbouring villages. Their departure didn't affect the local community to the same degree.

The bus rolled through the midlands to the sound of music and song, joy and laughter. Flasks of hot tea and sandwiches were shared around. A young married couple sat at the rear of the bus wrapped in each other's arms, unaware of the commotion.

Dusk was falling as we reached Blackhall. One of the obstacles we first encountered was lack of electricity. Rural electrification had not reached Blackhall. This was one of the luxuries we had become accustomed to in Mayo, but the friendly men employed by the Land Commission put a glow in our new homes with bright candles and warm fires.

At the break of dawn on St. Patrick's Day the children got their first view of their new surroundings. Our parents had painted a much brighter picture of our new homes than what we now experienced. With the innocence of youth I had expected a mature garden, "a fine garden to the front" our parents had told us. The reality was a barbed wire fence dividing the field around the house from the road; our surroundings looked bare and barren.

Despite some initial disappointments for us children our parents were delighted with their new farms. The big green fields were a far cry from the rocks and stones that covered our small patches of land that were scattered on four roads around the village of Woods.

The Dowling family of Ballybarney and the O'Connor family of Blackhall were the first families to offer the hand of friendship on the first day after our arrival. They took us to Calverstown and introduced us to other children of our age in the locality.

SOCIAL LIFE

Meanwhile our parents were busy sorting out which school we would attend. Ballymount was chosen by the majority, mostly because it was the school in the parish. Some opted for Ballyshannon but later changed to Ballymount. School in Ballymount also meant "To school through the fields". Wellington boots had to be worn, changed at the stile as we reached the bog road and hidden underneath a tree to be retrieved on the way home. Joe Dowling (RIP) often relieved the long trip with a lift in his already overcrowded car.

The next big decision was whether or not to become a dairy farmer. It was the only line of farming that was going to bring in a monthly cheque. Cowsheds and dairies were prepared, bons were bought and quotas sought. By October the first churns of milk were supplied to Sutton's Dairies. This was the business that was to provide a living for the migrant families for the next 40 years or more. Mick Gorman was the last man in Blackhall to supply milk to Premier Dairies (as it is now known) in 2002.

Sometimes the dairy farmers of Blackhall had to supplement their income by the occasional trip back to England or even further (my father went to Canada) for work on building sites or underground tunnels, while the wives still looked after the family and farm. They coped very well. I think the women of this era were the driving force behind the men.

After we settled in Blackhall the hand of friendship was extended by most locals. There were a few small farmers who resented migrants getting land. There were also the few cruel remarks when the children started school in Ballymount, some snide sneering remarks by some families referring to the newcomers as the "culchies".

Those attitudes were in the minority. There were a lot of positive gestures extended by the local community. Don Nolan (RIP), farm manager to the Lee Sisters, Bullhill, was always available to give advice on animal husbandry. Mick and Bridie Cassidy, Ballybarney, came to kill and cure the pig a few times.

The Breen family from Calverstown introduced us to céile dancing in Calverstown Hall under the direction of Pat Cosgrove. The friendly football matches between Blackhall and Calverstown were always memorable occasions. Jimmy Cassidy, in his Ford Prefect, took the women to Mass in Kilcullen. Local shopkeepers played a large part in the lives of the migrant farmers. They extended credit facilities. Hickey's of Calverstown, Kelly's of Narraghmore, Jim O' Connell, the Travelling Shop from Kilcullen. These are some of the people that are most vivid in my mind that helped us survive these early years.

The original settlers in Blackhall were;

1. Mick and Kathleen Walsh, Mick's mother Mary. They later had two sons. Mick and Kathleen died in mid-life.

2. Mary Lavin and two adult sons Charlie and Michael. Charlie married a local girl, Betty Cassidy and they had

SOCIAL LIFE

John Joe & Tommy Walsh 1951

five children. Michael married Mary Nolan and went to live in England. Mary died in her late 90s and was brought back to Mayo for burial.

3. John and Delia Byrne and four children; Tom, Seán, Mary and Kathleen. They later had two more daughters Carmel and Ann. John's elderly parents Dominic and Bridgid also made the move. *see picture on previous pages.*

4. Pat and Anne Gorman and their five children; Tom, Mary, Pat, Christine and Nancy. They later had six more children, Tony, Michael, Margaret, Eileen, Noreen and Siobhan.

5. Paddy and Mary Brennan and three children; Patricia, Mary and Frank and Paddy's mother Mary. The Brennans sold their farm in 1996 and bought another farm in Ballysax, the Curragh. They now live in Kilcullen town.

6. Michael and Delia Lavin and four children; Patricia, Martina, Michael and Anne. They later had two sons Tom and John. Michael's mother Brigid died in the early 60s and was brought back to Mayo for burial.

7. Tom and Mary Ellen Walsh and five sons; John Joe, Paddy, Tommy, Michael and Jim. They later had two more children Tony and Maureen.

The last 10 years saw the loss of a number of the original settlers. Tom and Mary Ellen Walsh, John and Delia Byrne, Michael Lavin, Pat Gorman (Snr), Michael and Kathleen Walsh died in mid-life. Some of the younger generation were taken from us in the prime of life. Tony Walsh (22) died in a tragic accident. In 1976 Pat Gorman, Snr, suffered a heart attack and died leaving a wife and two young children.

SOCIAL LIFE

May all of their souls rest in peace. We have three of the original settlers still living in Blackhall. Charlie Lavin, Anne Gorman and Delia Lavin. Paddy and Mary Brennan live heartily in the town of Kilcullen.

The first generation settlers worked and toiled on the land, reared and educated large families. Their children played a very active role in their local community. They went on to secondary school, joined clubs and organisations in the area such as Ballyshannon Macra na Feirme, Ballyshannon Macra na Tuaithe and Ballitore Juvenile Boxing Club. They became involved in school and church events in Crookstown parish from being altar severs back in 1956 to organising major fund raising for the church restoration fund in 2003 and many more activities in the intervening years.

The organisation that gained most from those second generation migrants was St. Laurence's G.F.C. John Joe Walsh has been associated with St. Laurence's since the late 1950s. John Joe was a student in St. Nathys College in 1956 when the move to Blackhall took place. It was there he acquired his love of Gaelic football. John Joe is still as passionate today for St. Laurence's as he was when the blood of youth ran through his veins in 1956. He has the distinction of having worn a county jersey for three counties, Mayo, Westmeath and Kildare.

Tony and Mick Gorman joined St. Laurence's as underage players in the mid 1960s and were a stalwart force on the team for a number of years. Mick wore the Lilywhite jersey in minor, under 21 right up to senior level.

Anne Kearney, Tom Byrne, Mick Gorman, Tony Gorman and John Joe Walsh have each played a major role as officers of the club, together with many more fine dedicated individuals in the locality, in the development of St. Laurence's football and clubrooms at Old Grange.

Blackhall has seen many changes over the years. Families grew up and settled down. Some married locals and settled down in the area. Others got sites on the family farm and built their houses in Blackhall, while some opted to cross the Irish Sea and Atlantic Ocean and settled abroad.

There are now 23 houses on the road that housed seven families in 1956 and a further 10 houses on the Calverstown to Narraghmore road which is referred to as Blackhall Upper.

Kildare has been good to the migrant farmers in Blackhall. In return I feel their children have given a good service of commitment and locality to their community, their parish and their county of adoption.

Mayo by birth, Kildare by adoption.... A marriage made in heaven!

SOCIAL LIFE

Memories from Crookstown

By Michael Delaney

Fun on the river at Crookstown Bridge

The site of the Church of St Laurence O'Toole in the parish of Narraghmore has been in existence for centuries. The interior has three aisles, belfry and an organ loft, a marble altar and a carved wooden pulpit outside the altar rails. Stained glass windows provide a very fitting background for the magnificent marble altar. A feature of the times ensured that separate aisles were provided for the men and women on either side of the main centre aisle. The lighting was provided by oil lamps and candles. A two-week mission, one for the men and one for the women, was part of the yearly calendar. Two missionaries conducted the twice-daily service. This was the time before lay readers or Eucharistic ministers. Only altar boys were allowed to play a role in any of the church ceremonies.

The river Griese flows calmly on its winding way, part of which is diverted to a millrace to power Crookstown corn and flour mill half a mile away. Corn drying and crushing were part of the mill's daily routine. It now functions as a tourist attraction and the milling process is demonstrated as a special treat for visitors and tourists. Good fishing and swimming in summer

SOCIAL LIFE

were part of the river's great attractions.

Girls and boys from the whole parish attended the national school at Crookstown. Motor transport, in the form of a school brake, was provided to transport the children from the outer regions to school and home again five days a week. There were no free lunches and a subscription was paid to cover heating costs.

On completion of their education at 14-years-of-age the girls and boys had to find employment locally or relocate to Dublin, England or America to help support their families. Most of the employment at home was outdoors and the days were long and cold in winter.

A local farmyard had a unique mechanism for churning butter. A horse, harnessed to a long beam, walked in circles turning gears to rotate the churn, causing a very distinctive sound that was heard for miles around the area.

A pub stood at Crookstown Cross on the Dublin-Carlow road. Mahoney Byrne was the landlord and the licence allowed him to sell porter, beer, wine, whiskey and cigarettes. Customers had to travel a distance of three miles on Sunday to be entitled to service as it was a 'bone fides' house. This meant that no local person could wet his whistle on the premises.

After being a farmer's boy for some years my thoughts were turning to machinery and technology. The 1939-45 war had ended and things began to change for the better in the locality. A distinguished gentleman, Jack O'Gorman, had purchased premises at Crookstown Cross in 1939 and had established a tillage contracting business. Jack was a man of the steam era and was a qualified motor engineer. He was an inventive genius and a very diligent worker. All his contracts were based on the power of Fordson tractors fuelled by TVO costing 2d per gallon. Night was transformed into day by electric lamps so threshing continued into the early morning hours. The threshing engines, once up and running, were a marvel of mechanical energy, thus the expression 'now you're threshing!' meant one was fully energized and active.

I was very fortunate to be Jack's understudy for a number of years. He involved me in all his projects and plans. We made tractor trailers and fitted pneumatic tyres to all the farmers' tractors so they could drive them to Mass on Sundays. The technical era improved the design and power of tractors and the new fuel was diesel.

Jack O'Gorman and his family opened a filling station and shop in 1946 and outside on the forecourt was parked their very own private aeroplane, a Westland Lysander Mark 2, formerly an Irish Air Corps reconnaissance plane. It stood proudly there for many years attracting a great deal of attention and enticing a number of customers to the O'Gorman business. Sadly it was neglected and only its propeller remains intact, now in the care of the late Jack's eldest son. Many photographs were taken of that plane and I am sure some are still in existence.

A petrol service station and garage with all the modern facilities is still in operation at Crookstown Cross under

SOCIAL LIFE

the ownership of Mr Seamus O'Reilly. In 1948 the rural electrification scheme reached the area. It made a huge difference to the quality of life. Nobody was ever in the dark again. The year 1950 saw me aspire to a higher level of technology in the now rapidly developing motor business. A full apprenticeship was served and qualifications procured from a very renowned garage in Castledermot.

During my years in Crookstown my social life was very good and by this time my mode of transport had progressed to a motorbike and then my very first car, a Ford 8 Model Y. I travelled all over the country as petrol was only 11.5 pence per gallon. My social life centred mainly around dancing. All the girls were beautiful.

Although I was working five and a half days every week my wages weren't great and I now had to run a car, dress myself and pay my mother whatever I could. I had very little left to treat my lady friends to milk shakes. My future had to be given serious consideration so I moved to Dublin to find employment and pursue my ambition to advance in automobile and aviation engineering. Some hard decisions had to be made; leave my family, friends and native village and sell my lovely car. Since I had not a bob to my name, the decision was made.

I left towards the end of 1955 and have returned to Ballitore on regular trips. I often wonder why I left, regardless of my success in achieving my ambitions and having had a very happy and successful life in Dublin. This area holds very many memories for me.

Scout leaders in Crookstown - 2000

SOCIAL LIFE

Memories Of A Life Well Lived

By John Duffy

When I was a child we paid regular visits to Ballymount, about 10 miles from where we lived on the Green Road, the Curragh. The purpose of this was to visit Maggie Dwyer, who appeared very old to our young eyes. Maggie was not related to us. She, and her brother John, were at this time old IRA people. When my father left his own home, on account of his own IRA leanings, which did not suit the rest of his family, Maggie Dwyer and her brother gave my father a roof over his head. He left home after many rows and never went home again. If he met his mother out walking and she was on her own, he would stop and talk to her for a few minutes. He stayed in Dwyer's for years, working the 20 acres of land they owned and later served as an officer in the Irish army.

My father served a couple of terms in jail for his IRA activities. He was sentenced to three years in the Glasshouse on the Curragh. He escaped from Newbridge prison during a separate sentence with about 20 others. They escaped through a sewer pipe going into the Liffey. Among his comrades were Tom Harris who later served as a Fianna Fáil TD for Kildare for many years, and Tom Flood, who by a strange coincidence had a daughter named Bridie, my wife now for over 30 years.

We often stayed overnight in Dwyer's and Maggie allowed us children the run of the place. My mother would visit her sister, who was married to James Humphries, who was teaching in Ballymount National School.

One morning Maggie was found in the yard after suffering a stroke and she died that evening. Very shortly after we moved to Ballymount, about June 1946. We lived close to the school and were able to come home for our lunch.

My father had decided to leave the army and he was retired on medical grounds. He loved Ballymount and made many improvements to the place. Not so my mother who had to endure life without electricity and running water, things we had taken for granted when living on the Curragh. We killed our own pig and cured the bacon by walking the salt into it. Joe Doyle was the butcher and we got a lot of help from neighbours in shaving the dead pig. We shared the meat with the neighbours, just as they did when they killed their pig.

In June 1947 my father fell ill again and was visited by Dr Shaughnessy of Ballitore who said he would have to go to the Mater Hospital in Dublin. While the preparations were being made my father called by brother Cathal to his room for a private chat with him. Then it was my turn. He told me as Cathal was delicate it might be my job to look

SOCIAL LIFE

John Duffy with Charlie Lavin on the Millenium Walk

after my mother Elizabeth if anything should happen to him in the future. Cathal was 11 and a half, I was 10 and Bernadette was 8. He had his little chat with Bernadette, then my mother, then away with the doctor to Dublin. He was dead by the time my mother visited the next day. Only for our neighbours, the Doyles, Dowlings, Hallorans and Connors we were lost. They helped to save our crops and thresh them. We hired Paddy Conon to dig out the potatoes and we picked them. The family car was sold as we could not afford to run it. This was the low time in our lives, with no electricity, no running water, toilet or bathroom.

Cathal would go to Meredith's to drive the tractor even though he was only about 12 years old. This brought in a welcome few pounds. Cathal also had a flair for buying and selling cattle and at 12 years of age was more than a match for many of the farmers and fellow dealers. Dunlavin, Baltinglass, Naas, Kildare and Blessington, were all fairs that were within walking distance.

At this time the horse and creel were in action so he could buy a calf or a litter of pigs, put them in the creel, sit up and let the cattle wander along in the dark 'til he got home. I hated going to the fairs and wished he'd sell to the first buyer so we could get home but that was not his method.

The first price quoted was always above what he would take and it was only after several heated exchanges, hand slappings, interventions by friends from both sides that a deal was struck.

When I was 14 Kildare County Council were carrying out improvements to the road at Ballymount Chapel which meant taking away a piece of our land. The fact that it was only a rocky piece of bad land made no difference and my mother was offered a job for me and our horse as a carter on the road. The fact that the original carter's horse had run away and broken the cart may have had something to do with the matter.

I started work on October 16, 1951. Hours of work were 8.20am to 5.30pm with a half hour break at 1pm and a short break around 10am. My wages were £5-15-6 and the only deductions were to the union.

For the first couple of months I could come home for my dinner but as the worked moved further away from home I brought my billy can with me. This can was put with about 20 others to boil on the fire. To stop the tea from getting smoky the trick was to put a stick in the boiling water. I don't know if it worked or not as the tea was that strong that a bit of smoke would not be noticed.

My horse did not really have the temperament for working on the road and was more suited to working on a farm. This horse was a vicious biter and I very rarely ventured within reach of her head and most time I steered her with the reins. Children walking to and from school were always a worry for me as telling them the horse was wicked did not deter them from going quite close to her. I knew by the white in her eye when it was time to interfere. I got a few bites myself in my time, the most serious being when she caught my leg and left me with my trousers torn from the waistband to the turnup on the bottom.

During my time with the council I worked with Jim Maguire of Brewel. Another man I worked with was Tom Keating, a very decent man of about 68 years of age who was in the British army in his youth. He was in India when the troubles started in Ireland.

One time while working in a gravel pit we did not have a watch among us. He put a piece of stick about 18" long standing in sand and drew a circle around it, then divided the circle into quarters and made an estimate of the time, a skill he had learned while serving in India.

He lived on his own as his sister had been killed crossing the road in Ballyshannon some years earlier. I can still see him with an old string shopping bag hanging on the bike. His cap was always black and scorched, a sure sign of a bachelor as the cap was used for lifting the kettle off the crane over the open fire.

Another man whom I remember from my days with the Kilcullen gang was Tom Cullen. After about three and a half years I got fed up on the road as most of the men were much older than me so I quit the roadwork and took a factory job in Santry in Dublin repairing vacuum cleaners. The job was ok but I didn't like Dublin and came home every weekend and I left after a year. I was looking for a job when I heard there were roadworks starting at Blackrath. My uncle Louis knew the ganger Tom Hipwell and he recommended me as a carter and I started the next day.

I have great memories of working with the Moone gang as the atmosphere was quite different with these men, a mixture of young and old and lots of craic. Owen Kelly, Johnnie Toole, Nick Murphy, Joe Foley, Bill Brown and Joe Brennan are those I remember from that period. I worked on the Moone section for about three years. As work was sometimes slack I could find myself at home for a month at a time. Coming up to Christmas schemes were started to give work to people who had no job. This relief work involved cleaning river and big drains. I would be sent to the council yard in Newbridge for a supply of shovels, boots and cement to repair bridges on the

SOCIAL LIFE

John, Bernadette and Cathal Duffy circa 1944

SOCIAL LIFE

scheme. During one of these period of slackness I got a job as a labourer and tractor driver with a local builder, Eddie Nolan, who was building 11 houses in south Kildare. I also started doing a bit of plastering.

I worked for a few months with Dublin plasterers doing the outside of Ballymount Church with lads by the name of Carroll, brothers of a former Lord Mayor of Dublin. The height of the building never bothered me as I was young at the time and working at the belfry was no problem. We hacked off all the old plaster to the stone, skudded it then a scratch coat of plaster and then the dashing. Pads Connor of Brewel, Paddy Ward of Brewel, Joe Halloran of Blackrath and myself and the Carrolls did this job. Years later I worked with Peter McEnroe and his gang plastering the inside of the same building. This time someone else was doing the mixing as I was plastering. Still on laborer's wages.

The next years saw me working in the Ropes factory in Newbridge, with Larry Moran putting bodies on trailers, and in the rubber factory in Kilcullen. As the factory had nearly closed completely due to shortage of work I was let go. In the previous few years I had bought more sheep and cattle and was independent of the factory. I also did some work with Mick Cardiff on different jobs around the country.

When things got quiet around Christmas I would stay at home while the cows were calving and the ewes, yeaning. The rest of the year I would do the few jobs at home before going to work . I also did farm work for Ken Millar driving tractors and looking after sheep. During my time with him some land nearby was taken over by the Land Commission and we got 27 acres. We surrendered six acres of good land in Crookstown and got 10 acres of wet land in its place. This land nearer to home was a big advantage, plus the 17 acres at a rent of £66 per year for 25 years. This allowed us to keep more livestock. When Bridie's father died he left her 15 more acres.

Apart from my worklife I still had time for lots of enjoyment. The pictures in Kilcullen once a week and sometimes twice a week were my outlet for a long time. On the bicycle the six miles took less than half an hour and when I got my NSU it only took 10 minutes. Lots of westerns and newsreels were the standard fare in those days. James Cagney and Edward G Robinson were the stars of the gangster films and others I remember were Humphrey Bogart and Lauren Bacall. I also went to the pictures in Connor's barn in Ballitore.

The surroundings were not as fancy as those in Kilcullen but that did not matter. Dances were held in the Immal Hall in Dunlavin, the Little Theatre in Crookstown, the John F K in Kilcullen, Macra na feirme in Ballyshannon and the Dreamland in Athy.

Joe Doyle and myself danced with two sisters who were with our group on one of these excursions in the Mayfair ballroom in Kilkenny. John and Una were an item for that night only whereas myself and Bridie are still an item after over 30 years. We were married in 1970 and have raised nine children.

SOCIAL LIFE

John, Bernadette and Cathal Duffy circa 1944

SOCIAL LIFE

Narraghmore Parish Credit Union

By Pauline Mooney

In 1966 a study group held a meeting to form Narraghmore Parish Credit Union. The idea of the union for the parish emanated from the Very Rev. J Moynihan, PP. The union was affiliated to the Irish League of Credit Unions in September 1969.

The chairman was Very Rev. Moynihan and the committee was comprised of Sam Sloane, then Principal of Ballymount National School, the late Ned Ball, Narraghmore, Rita Mooney, Crookstown and her daughter Margie, now Mrs O'Connell.

The purpose of the credit union is to promote thrift among its members by affording them the opportunity of accumulating their savings and to create for them a source of credit, for provident and productive purposes, at fair and reasonable rates of interest and to provide the opportunity for the members to use and control their money for mutual benefit.

The Board of Directors appointed a credit committee of three members, Mrs C O'Mara, Mrs Mc McCarthy and Mrs R Mooney to consider and decide on applications for loans. Some of the earliest loans amounted to £10, £20, £40 and even £50. It was proposed that the credit union be held in the church vestry after Mass each Sunday. There were 105 loans granted during 1971 to the value of £5,375. The purpose of the loans were household, land reclamation, home improvements, fuel, hay, straw and turf.

Today the credit union continues to provide a vital service for and by the local community.

Enjoying the atmosphere of a Narraghmore/Ballytore Senior Citizens Christmas Party in Kelly of Narraghmore were Sr. Anne Maureen Kidd, Mary Hickey and Peg Donovan.

Photo by Michael O'Rourke.

SOCIAL LIFE

NARRAGHMORE GROUP WATER SCHEME

By Mark Wright and Christopher Heffernan

The Narraghmore Group Water Scheme was originally the brainchild of Rev. Fr. Moynihan P.P. of Crookstown who organised a meeting on September 3, 1970. The idea was to supply fresh water to all the houses in Narraghmore and the surrounding area, roughly 30 square miles. Trustees elected at the meeting included John Donovan, Robert Jackson, Christopher Heffernan and Garrett Yates. The water was eventually put into houses in 1974. The scheme cost £80,000 in total; the Department of the Environment provided £26,000, the balance, £54,000, was raised locally.

The scheme originally served 135 houses and 60 field connections, with five pumps at The Seven Wells filling an 85,000-gallon reservoir on top of Nine Tree Hill, that gave gravity flow to all areas.

The system worked well enough for the first 12 to 15 years but then the strain began to tell. The number of connections had doubled at this stage and wear and tear was beginning to show. For the next seven or eight years it was a nightmare trying to keep the pumps going and the reservoir was also leaking badly. In the mid '90s a big programme was started to upgrade pumps, cover wells, put a new reservoir on Nine Tree Hill and repair the old one. At this stage we needed some help to get the best grants available.

We called in Jack Wall who drew up a plan and presented it to the then Minister for the Environment, Brendan Howlin. The outcome was £28,000 for a new reservoir, it cost £35,000 plus VAT, repair of old reservoir £12,000, a water level monitor £6,000, new pumps £7,000, three phase electricity £12,000, well covers £1,500.

There was a new panel and switchboard installed some years earlier. We now have about 350 houses on the scheme and with new equipment life is much easier. We have changed the name to Narraghmore Group Water Scheme Ltd. for insurance purposes. We had to have seven trustees to comply with limited company rules. They are as follows: Kathleen Hickey, Narraghmore; Barry Kelly, Narraghmore; Don Ashmore, Mullaghmast, Ballitore; Christopher Heffernan, "Lynam's Garden", Ballitore; George Hendy, Nine Tree Hill, Ballitore; Vincent Gorman, Ballindrum, Athy; Mark Wright, "The Decoy", Ballitore.

Robert Jackson (RIP), was a long serving trustee. He made a very valuable contribution and his passing in February 2000 was deeply regretted. We hope to keep serving the area with good clean water to the best of our ability in the years ahead.

SOCIAL LIFE

Lord Edward's Own Pipe Band

By Billy Donovan

Lord Edward's own Pipe Band was formed in 1916 and its membership was drawn mostly from the old IRA.
The band hall was in John Flanagan's barn at the Seven Stars. The barn was often raided by the Black n' Tans and there was a picture of a Black n' Tan drawn on the gable wall of the building.

The band's first outing was to a sports day in Kyledoon in 1918. In 1920 the band attended a meeting in Naas which was broken up by the auxiliaries and a banner with Erin go Brá written on it was taken and never returned. This banner had earlier been presented by a Mr Biggers from Belfast.

Some time later some of the band's instruments were taken by a rival band and when band members decided to go and retrieve them they were warned of an ambush and decided against making the journey.

Ginger Kenny and Tommy Hanlon joined the band around 1923/24 and remained life long members. In 1925 the band played at the bazaar in Crookstown. Mick O'Toole was in charge at this time.

In 1928 they played at a sports meeting in Kilgowan. On a visit to Kill in 1930 they had such a good time that one of the banners was left behind and Ginger Kenny had to collect it next morning on his way to Dublin.

Elections were a busy time for the band as all parties engaged them to encourage their followers.
During the Emergency years the band activities were severely curtailed and all the local bands were in the same position.

After the Emergency Ginger Kenny took over as Pipe Major. One of the highlights of the band's year was the annual pilgrimage to St Patrick's Well when they played, starting in the village of Narraghmore. Over the years the band took part in many competitions, including those in Castledermot, Harold's Cross and Tullamore where they won many prizes.

Jack O Connor became Pipe Major in 1960 and the Narraghmore band was registered with the Irish Pipe Band Association. They competed in the World Pipe Band contest in Belfast in June 1962. This meant setting off at 3am and having special arrangements with the customs for early morning clearance at the border at 7am.

Louie Noble designed the crest on the belt buckle. This crest has been much admired over the years.

Tim Keogh started to train the band in the 1960s and John Keogh trained the drummers. During these years the

SOCIAL LIFE

band competed in many competitions in Scotland with Jack O Connor as Pipe Major. He won the Pipe Major Award in 1970.

In 1968 the band won the all Ireland championship in grade four. The members that year were Andy O'Connor, Jack O'Connor, Billy Donovan, Anthony Donovan, pipers, Tommy Moore, Jimmy Byrne, Ned Byrne, bass drums, Jim O'Connor, staff major, Johnny Keogh, drum sergeant, Ann and Nuala Keogh, drum corps.

In 1961 the band won first prize in the miniature band section under Irish Pipe Band Association rules. The members that day were Tim Keogh, instructor, Jack O'Connor, Andy O'Connor, pipers, Billy Donovan, Ned Byrne, bass drums, Bob O'Connor and James Neavy, drums.

Over the years Jack O'Connor won many awards including second place in the piob uileann section of Fleadh Laighean in 1995 and second place in the slow airs section in the All Ireland and third place in the piob uileann section at the Fleadh na hEireann in the same year.

In 1991 the members of Lord Edward's Own Pipe Band, Narraghmore, marched proudly down Fifth Avenue in New York to take part in the annual St Patrick's Day Parade.

The Pipe Band in Crookstown 1960's

SOCIAL LIFE

Reflections from Inchaquire

By Michael Delaney

Inchaquire, a townland on the Kilcullen to Carlow road, is about two files north of Ballitore, an area that was mostly self sufficient in the early part of the 20th century.

A cotton mill, owned by the Green family, was situated on the river Griese at Inchaquire and processed the flax grown locally on Spratstown uplands. It was harvested by local labour, pulled manually and taken to the mill for processing into cotton, which had a good commercial value. The company built a dwelling complex near the mill for its workers. It was known as the Factory Yard.

There was also a local bakery called Finn's bakery and bread was delivered locally by a horse drawing a large bread van with the driver sitting on top. Finn's also had their own blacksmith forge and farrier facility so all their horses were always well shod.

A couple of very good carpenter's shops also served a wide area, providing all the farmers' requirements, such as farm carts, drays, wheelbarrows, gates, ladders and so forth. They also supplied all the coffins to the funeral undertakers in the locality.

The timber was native and the work of sawing, shaping and finishing was done using hand tools. Wheels were also produced by hand tools and shod with iron bands. This was quite a complicated procedure that relied on craftsmanship and experience.

Some modern industry still exists in the area, Inchaquire Industries, established by an enterprising local family that supply all the tools and machinery to meet present day requirements. This industry is on the location of the original Finn's bakery.

Road bowling was a popular sport in those days. Contestants had to throw an iron ball, about the size of a tennis ball, along the centre of a road with a straight section a couple of miles long. Teams competed and the team to complete the distance with the fewest number of throws won the contest.

Swimming in the Griese was very popular and a very deep pool was created by damming the river at specific locations. Skittles and nine holes were also popular.

Pitch and toss was also very much in favour. A two-headed penny could be an asset as the evening grew dim. Cock fighting and dog coursing were also part of the local social scene. Dog and cock fights were illegal and cruel and meets were secretly arranged at which large bets were won and lost.

A row of dwellings called Posey Park accommodated 14 families. Each had a

SOCIAL LIFE

large garden where all the vegetables the family needed were produced.

There was a fife and drum band founded in the area in the early 20th century. It had a large membership and met and rehearsed on a regular basis. Young and new members were recruited and trained and outings were organised in the summer months to such places as Poulaphouca, to perform at football matches. Transport for the band was by local jarvies and their jaunting cars that accommodated the band members and their instruments.

Audio tapes of the customs, pastimes and lifestyle or local characters are available and some of the band instruments still exist in reasonable condition. Fife and drum bands also existed in Mullaghmast, Belan and Brewel. Some of the bands were comprised of families and friends.

My father was a member of the Inchaquire band and lived in the Factory Yard. I was born there and spent my first three years there until the family moved to the Glebe at Crookstown Lower. My father became a livestock herdsman for a local farmer who lived on his other farm, some miles away. We had total freedom on 100 acres fully stocked with all kinds of animals that had to be cared for seven days a week.

We had lots of lessons about nature and enjoyed every minute. I attended school in Crookstown where I received my formal education. The teachers were Mr O'Connor, principal, and Mr Flannery, assistant, and as primary school teachers, they were very professional and gave each pupil every chance to be knowledgeable and good citizens. The seven years spent there were fruitful and happy and my education was then complete. In those days children did not start school until they were seven years of age.

The dwellings in the Factory Yard were converted to a large modern house which has been occupied by the same family for many years.

A branch of the railway line ran two and a half miles away at Colbinstown. This line ran from Dublin to Tullow in County Carlow. All livestock and freight to and from Dublin was sent by rail. This was a great lifeline for the area as road transport was virtually non-existent and all livestock had to be driven along the road to local fairs. This meant starting out at 3am to walk eight or nine miles to local fairs at Baltinglass, Dunlavin, Athy or Kilcullen, requiring good boots and a lot of stamina.

Crookstown N.S. teachers, Mr & Mrs O'Connor with their two sons.

SOCIAL LIFE

THE GOAT HOUSE

By Bill Mackey

The Goat House opened after the Spout Hall closed about 1928. It was originally built as a band room. The Goat House was located at Crandoon, Glasshealy. It had oil lamps for lighting. The roof and sides were galvanise and there was a timber floor in it. Dances were held every Sunday night and admission was 6d (old pence). Dances started at 9pm and went on until around 12 midnight. Music was provided by a local band. Band members included Tom Browne, Pat Doyle, John Byrne, Jim Byrne, Owen Kelly and Kevin Byrne. The MCs were Tom Browne, Pat Doyle and Peter Kane. Mrs. Byrne provided tea and sandwiches for a small fee. The Goat House would have held between 30 and 40 people. People travelled from Nurney, Kilkea, Ballitore and Moone to the Goat House. The only means of transport in those days was by bicycle. The Goat House closed around 1946. Many a man met his future wife there. The Goat House was also known as "The Tibley" and "The Bzonk".

School performance at the Little Theatre.

The Little Theatre

By John Duffy

The Little Theatre holds a special place in all our hearts and is it any wonder?

The Little Theatre has had many a glorious hour in its long career and none finer than when Mass was celebrated there during the renovation of the parish church.

Many events were held in the Little Theatre down through the years. We all remember bingo sessions held on a regular basis for years but I was thinking back to the days when we had Jimmy Dunney here for the big dances. Other well-known bands to grace the stage were the Gallowglass and the Ardellis ceilidh bands for the Irish dances and the Red Aces, The Breakaways and Joe O'Neill's Stardust and many more.

Many big socials were run to raise parish funds or to help special cases of hardship when families were down on their luck.

Then we had the 'send off' social for the newly ordained priest or nun from the parish when a few pounds would be raised and presented to them on the happy occasion.

Films were also shown in the Little Theatre and it also played host to the travelling shows and the amateur dramatic society productions. Lots of local artists took their first bows from the stage of the Little Theatre and these performances were generally very well received. Dublin artists such as Albert Healy, Monica Bonnie, and Charlie Byrne performed here. It was here that I had my first dance with Bridie Flood, who was to become my wife, so it holds many happy memories for us.

Who can forget the big card drives billed as the biggest in Ireland at the time? The old school classrooms were used as cloakrooms and supper rooms and still they had to erect tents in the schoolyard to accommodate the huge crowds who attended. The Little Theatre was attached to the school which branched out right and left, boys on one side, girls on the other. This cruciform shape was the old chapel built in 1720 and was in continuous use until 1864. Cardinal Cullen administered the sacrament of Confirmation here to 197 children on August 7, 1854, ten years before the new church was built.

In 1864 the new church was opened and this must have been an important day in the life of the parish. A new graveyard beside that church was also opened around the same time. The first person interred in the graveyard on January 4, 1866, was Thomas Kelly, Ballymount, who was aged 77 years. The last of that family interred there

SOCIAL LIFE

was Lizzie Kelly, Feb 13, 1959, aged 80 years. The Kelly family lived where Tallon's of Ballymount now live.

Around the Little Theatre building, where we park our cars, was the graveyard for the old church. Those big old gravestones that are placed along the wall in the present old graveyard were removed from around the Little Theatre building.

The building, known as the Little Theatre has served the parish and community since 1720 as a church, theatre and community centre.

I believe old buildings retain some little part of the people and events that have passed through them and if you just listen to them they will tell us many truths about ourselves.

Our own lives are very short when measured against buildings of the age of the Little Theatre.

BALLYSHANNON DRAMATIC SOCIETY, 1944

Back Row (left to Right) - John McNamee, Arthur Hendy, Peter Smith, Pat Morrin, Matt Doyle, Peter Toole, Jimmy Keiran

Front Row: Eileen M. Dowling, Eileen B. Dowling, Denis Morrin, Moira Winters, Dick Price, Agnes Dowling

SOCIAL LIFE

THE THRESHING

By John Duffy

"God speed the plough grow more wheat". That was a common prayer during the Emergency years of 1939 to 1945 when Ireland had to grow all her own food. During these years the people were very aware of their dependence on the plough and the soil to keep hunger from our shores. Nowadays walk into any supermarket and look at the variety of food on offer from different countries and you have to marvel at this change. Still, wherever this food is produced it is soil, a farmer and God almighty, that are involved in the process. The farmer may have 10,000 acres or the meat may come from a herd of 1,000 cattle. Nonetheless we are still dependent on this wholesome food for our survival.

Looking back over the years we always think of the threshing as the highlight of the year's work, but a lot of work went ahead of the threshing. The plough working from October onwards 'til December, the job of tilling and sowing, the hope of a good harvest, the reaping, binding and gathering into ricks, all in preparation for the big day of the threshing.

The threshing mill and all the people who worked at the threshing travelled from one neighbour's farm to the next. The machine men were looked on with awe. At that time anyone who understood machinery and had lots of grease on their clothes was given a special

Meal-time was an important part of the working day.

seat at the table, usually in the parlour, if the house had one. Most of the men and women who worked at the threshing were very glad of this work as they were paid at the end of the day's work, and were fed well.

Neighbours, who had already had their threshing, turned out to return the favour and at mealtime there could be 20 or more people to be fed. Plenty of spuds, a big piece of meat and cabbage were provided, followed by big servings of rice, lots of milk and big mugs of tea, the stronger the better. A plateful of spotted dog completed the meal, leaving everyone full and happy. As usual where you have a crowd the joker appears and this fellow helped to make life a lot more bearable and helped to lighten the burden of hard work. Around the table when all were settled into the dinner he would start getting on to the women serving,

SOCIAL LIFE

enquiring about their love lives and offering to fix them up with some of the young and not-so-young men around the table. Lots of joking and laughing followed, with the odd serious remark thrown in, because the reality was that perhaps it was himself the joker was thinking about. This was all taken in good spirits and helped to shorten the day.

The two Tommys, Tommy Murphy and Tommy Kenna were quiet and decent men. These men always carried the straw from the mill. To see them taking the big forks of straw as it fell from the mill and then hoist them onto their shoulders one would have to wonder how they stuck this work all day. It was not possible to see the man under the big forkful of straw, but this was their job and they preferred it to any other job at the threshing.

When the haggard quietened the farmer did his sums and counted up the bills he owed in his local shop. His hope was that when they were all paid he would have enough to see himself and his family through the winter and the spring when he would again be dependant on the generosity of the local shopkeepers.

One horse power was the order of the day.

SOCIAL LIFE

M. Wright with pals bringing in the hay

John McNamee & Step-brother James Gorman

SPORTS

BALLITORE GAME CLUB

By Willie Deacon

In 1966 a meeting of all rural organisations was held in Cahir. Involved were N.F.A., Bord Failte, Department of Lands, Macra na Feirme and many such groups. Game management and habitat development were identified as one of the most important schemes to proceed with in the countryside.

An organiser was appointed in each county. Ballitore was one of the first clubs formed in Kildare in 1969 and the officers were: Chairman, Mick Mahon; secretary, Pat Leigh; treasurers, Jim Hannon and Tommy Hendy. The club had around 25 members the first year but by the 1970 and '71 season membership had grown to 50. In the early years grants were paid for the rearing of pheasants, and a bounty on foxtails helped the game stocks.

Shoots were mostly clay pigeon as there was very little game in the countryside at that time. Willie Deacon got the traps and clay birds in Malahide and the first shoot was held in Kirwan's field in Ballitore. Further clay shoots were held in Deacon's farm over the years. These were open shoots and were often used as fund raising events for Narraghmore and Crookstown churches.

After some years Jim Fitzharris took over as secretary and he organised a lease of 15 years on a portion of Narraghmore Bog. This was later changed to a long-term lease on a greater portion of the bog. A lot of work and money was invested in the fencing and stocking of duck ponds, rearing pheasants and providing access into the bog. This was done with the help of Jim Fitzharris, Mick Conlon, Kevin Mooney and John and Francis Dowling. The long-term aim is to develop this as an amenity area for the club members and local residents.

This has developed well with grants from Irish Habitat Trust. Some years ago County Kildare Regional Game Council shoots were held in Kirwan's field in Ballitore. This was one of the biggest shoots ever held. 18,000 clay birds were used and clubs from all over Ireland were represented. Over £3,000 in prizes was on offer and Griffin & Hawe donated most of the prizes. Seven competitions were held, with members of the club looking after the shoot. Ballyroe Club also helped on the day. A donation was given to Narraghmore Church and Crookstown Church.

With over 50 members, the shooting access covers 270 farms and over 10,000 acres. With extensive game reserves at Narraghmore Bog and Battlemount Wood the future of this club looks very bright indeed. Ballitore Game Club is a member of Kildare Regional Game Council and affiliated to the N.A.R.G.C.

John Dempsey, ML Fitzsimons, Jim Fitzharris, Kevin Mooney, Rowney McCabe, Jim Hannon, Micko Doyle, John Doyle, Stan Connolly, Eddie Wright, Mick Conlan, Willie Deacon, Pat Byrne, Eddie Conway.

Camogie 1933-2003

By Matt and Patricia Doyle

The origins of camogie in Ballitore can probably be traced to a letter from Mrs Mary Kealy, proprietor of Kealy's Shop to Sheila Norton, Bricanna, Johnstown, County Kilkenny on August 30, 1930, regarding an interview for the position of shop assistant.

The interview must have been satisfactory as shortly afterwards Sheila Norton took up the position of shop assistant with Kealy's where she was to remain for almost 12 years. When the first camogie club was formed in Ballitore Sheila was elected captain and the club colours chosen were the black and amber of Kilkenny. A report in the Leinster Leader of March 31, 1934 states that a camogie club had been formed and that on the previous Sunday over 20 girls had taken part in the first practice in a field given free of charge by Mr E Kelly.

Late 1930s Ballitore Camogie Team:
Back Row (L to R): Kitty McCann (PP's Housekeeper), Liz Daly,
Masie Bolger, Theresa Farrell, Margaret Keatly
Middle Row (L to R): Liz Mackey, Mary Mackey, Patsy Casey, Kathy Daly, Nina Whelan
Front Row (L to R): Molly Rooney, Mary Casey, Peg Leigh

This seems to have been the first official outing of the club, although the reports of the 1933 camogie championship in the Leinster Leader states that Clane, Straffan, Castledermot and Ballitore took part with Castledermot emerging as winners!!

The next mention of the club is on July 7, 1934 when they travelled to Skerries for a friendly game and were beaten 5-1 to 0-0. It appears there were two camogie teams in the parish at the time. Friendly matches were the most common activity in the early years and it appears that some players transferred to Moone Club for a while. However it was reported on March 11, 1939, again in the Leinster Leader, that Ballitore Camogie Club had been revived after a lapse of a few years, thanks to the efforts of Miss S Norton, Miss T Farrell and a number of other ladies in the district. A general meeting was held and Miss Norton was elected captain, Miss Dotie Keatley, secretary and Miss K Kealy, treasurer. It was stated that there was reason to believe that the club would regain recognition as one of the leading clubs in the county as, with Miss Norton and other officials in control, success was assured.

The panel of players at that stage was: Molly Rooney, Mary Casey, Pat Leigh, Liz Mackey, Mary Mackey, Patsy Casey, Katy Daly, Nina Whelan, Liz Daly, Masie Bolger, Kitty McCann, Teresa Keatley, Margaret Keatley and Sheila Norton. This panel was added to by many others during the active years of the club; the Kirwan sisters, Moone, the Dempsey sisters, Kilmead, the Brady sisters, Usk, Sheila Park, Dunlavin and many others contributed to the club in those days.

In 1940 Ballitore reached the junior final having defeated Rathangan, Ellistown and Straffan. They played Athy in the final and the game ended in a draw, Ballitore 2 goals, Athy 2 goals. The replay was played at Mr Joseph Masterson's field in Kilmead.

The pitch was water-logged after heavy rain and the Athy team were the heavier and stronger side, an advantage that contributed to their victory. The play was not of a high standard generally but what it lacked in this respect was made up for by the sheer determination of the players. Ballitore had a fairly even share of the game but their forwards were very weak and missed several golden opportunities. Mary Casey was outstanding in goal, K. Dowling at fullback and Sheila Norton defended stubbornly. At midfield Josie Cogan did useful work against strong opposition and showed herself capable of holding her own with the very best. Her sister Nan, though not up to her usual form, put in some very effective play. Peg Leigh and Dotie Keatley were the best of the Ballitore forwards, with Dotie scoring their only goal. The final score was Ballitore 1-0, Athy 3-0. Ballitore was well represented at county level in the early 1940s. Dotie Keatley, Kathleen Mackey and Elizabeth Daly all wore the county jersey with distinction when the Kildare team reached the Leinster final in 1943.

Camogie faded out sometime in the mid '40s as girls got married and in those days that ended one's camogie

SPORTS

career. The club was reformed in February 1980 in the Ballitore/Kilmead area by Mrs Margaret Timmons and Mrs Celia White. Officers elected then included: chairperson, Kate Treacy; vice chairperson, Mrs Celia White; secretary, Patricia Keatley; assistant secretary, Deirdre Keatley; treasurer, Mrs Margaret Timmons; fund-raising organisers, Ann May Miley, Mrs Margaret Timmons; team captain Kate Treacy; team trainer Mrs Celia White.

Training was held in St Laurence's GAA grounds at Old Grange. Girls walked, jogged and cycled to attend under the watchful eye of team manager Mrs Cecila White. The colours chosen were the St Laurence's GAA colours; red/yellow culotte skirts and jerseys and red socks. The skirts were made by Myra O'Brien and Margaret Blanchfield. Camogie was one of the few outdoor sports for girls in the parish. The girls turned up for training in numbers which, in the first year in competition, were sufficient to field two teams, one of which reached the final of the league. In 1981 St Laurence's won the junior championship and the league. The following are that team that brought honour to themselves and their parish: Dolores Corcoran, Bridget Corcoran, Della Killeen, Rose Killeen, Martina Dempsey, Lil Byrne, Margaret Blanchfield, Patricia Keatley, Deirdre Keatley, Helen Fitzharris, Lily Lynam, Anna Lynam, Lucy King, Ann May Miley and Michelle Deegan.

In 1989 St Laurence's won their first

Old Grange aerial photo

SPORTS

*Members of all ten, Senior County Championship winning teams 1994-2003
Aisling Treacy, Roisin Walsh, Elaine Miley, Ruth Treacy, Naomi Treacy*

ever intermediate title when they defeated Carbury. Final score: St Laurence's 1-8 Carbury 2-3.

The early '90s saw the start of the club's golden years, which they are enjoying up to the present day. 1992 saw the senior team take to the field against Broadford in the county final. Broadford were going for their 11th title in a row. The young Larry's team were full of determination and played extremely well all through. Liz O'Donoghue was outstanding at full back, 14-year-old twins Ruth and Naomi Treacy, alongside their sister Aisling, played a major role in the team's victory. This was a first class effort from St Laurence's, eight of whom were under 18 players. This was the club's first ever senior title after having a clean sweep in the underage competition in 1991. Scorers for St Laurence's were A. Treacy (1-1), Martina Miley (1-0), Sharon Browne (0-2). Lucy O'Neill was the team captain and goalkeeper on this historic occasion. The senior team has now won 11 championships, of which 10 were in a row (1994-2003).

As Kildare champions St Laurence's won their first-ever Leinster final when they defeated Camross on home

SPORTS

ground on Sunday, August 4, 1996. It was a closely contested game of camogie with literally a puck of the ball between the sides throughout the match. A determined St Laurence's side, and a will to win, gave the Kildare team the title. The girls had realised their dream and in doing so had made history for their club.

The final score was St Laurence's 1-10, Camross 1-8. The team were Lucy O'Neill, Roisin Walsh, Kate Treacy, Melanie Treacy, Naomi Treacy, Patricia Doyle, Aisling Treacy, Ruth Treacy, Elaine Miley, Michelle Aspell, Sharon Browne and Margaret Butterfield. Subs: Deirdre McDonald, Ciara Tallon, Suzanne Keatley, Pamela Donovan and Patrica Aspell. This team was trained to a very high standard by Bernard Higgins, Ballitore.

The club has also enjoyed considerable success at underage level winning u13, u14, u15, u16, u18 and u21 titles. Camogie was introduced to Crookstown National School in the early 1990s and the school has been a nursery for the St Laurence's club. The school has won several titles, including the famous three-in-a-row Mini Sevens titles 1999, 2000 and 2001.

As a result of this competition Crookstown National School has had the privilege of providing several players for the Mini Games that take place

St. Laurence's U-14 Camogie Team - Kildare Feile Representatives Belfast 2002
Back Row (L to R): Manager Peter Barry, Aisling Russell, Laura Clifford, Lydia Byrne, Serena Kelly, Louise Keatley, Colma Reynolds, Laura Dunne, Caoimhe O'Halloran, Laura Whelan, Deirdre Burke, Sarah Delahunt, Selector Patricia Doyle
Front Row (L to R): Selector Lily Bowden, Pamela Lavin, Anne Marie Kearney, Emma Doyle, Margaret O'Neill, Lorraine Bowes (Capt), Orla Lawlor, Emma Dunne, Helen Mooney, Selector Deirdre McDonald,
missing from photo is Rhona Mulhall

SPORTS

at half-time during the Leinster and All Ireland hurling finals. Louise Keatley, Sharon Doyle, Helen Mooney, Lydia Byrne and Laura Mooney have all enjoyed the experience of playing before a full house in Croke Park, while still under 14, something about which most camogie players only get to dream.

Camogie was introduced to Scoil Mhicil Naofa by Lily Bowden, one of our own long serving members, and as a result of her dedication and commitment to the school the club now has a number of players from Athy. Long may this continue.

St Laurence's has always been well represented at county level, while a large number of players also hold Leinster medals: Melanie Treacy (3), Patricia Keatley (3), Aislilng Treacy (2), Liz O'Donoghue (2), Sharon Browne (1), Reiltin Treacy (1). All also hold All Ireland Junior Camogie Championship winners' medals. Playing with the Kildare county team they reached the first final in 1986, only to be defeated by a strong Clare side. They came back again in 1987 to win Kildare's first ever All Ireland in camogie, defeating Armagh. They were back again in 1989, this time defeating Galway after a replay in Birr. 1990 saw the Kildare team reach the All Ireland final for their fourth appearance in the final, this time defeating Tipperary. This is a feat yet to be achieved by the men!

The club is extremely lucky to have so many voluntary, dedicated, members willing to help with the everyday activities, both on and off the field. St Laurence's now fields teams at all levels and the club is recognised as one of the top ones in the county. With so many teams to be kitted out fundraising is ongoing.

Barry Kelly has been the club's main sponsor over the past decade. Other means of fundraising much needed cash has been done by the committee with auctions of promise, fancy dress, walks, raffles etc. The club is so lucky to have the use of the GAA's excellent facilities at Old Grange for, without them, camogie would struggle to survive.

The following are the elected officers for 2004: chairperson, Deirdre McDonald; vice chairperson, Patricia Doyle; secretary, Aisling Treacy; assistant secretary, Brenda Tallon; treasurer, Debherail Owens; assistant treasurer, Ruth Treacy; PRO Dermot Breen.

Our since thanks to all who made this brief history of camogie in the area possible. To Nina Darcy (RIP) who sadly died since the interviews for this article, Peg Deay and Theresa Doran, surviving members of the first team, for their memories, team photographs and background information. To Mario Corrigan and the Kildare County Library history section for his invaluable help and to the Leinster Leader for the use of their records.

If you or any member of your family was a member of that first camogie team in Ballitore we would like to hear from you. Please contact Matthew and Patrica Doyle, Blackrath, Colbinstown and help us complete the history of the club.

SPORTS

Horseracing and Associated Sports

By Paddy Doyle

Francis Flood (centre) with his son Tom, on his right is Larry Dunne with Garoupe - Winner of the Irish Grand National and on his left is Ronan McParland with Glencarrig Lady - Winner of the Cheltenham Gold Cup in 1972

It would be strange indeed, if a parish in the sporting county of Kildare, the head quarters of the horse racing industry, and the home of the Killing Kildare Fox Hounds, did not have its share of notable people involved in the sport of kings. Research has proved that many people were involved in making a living from the industry over the past century. Indeed this is not to be wondered at since we have three well-known and famous racecourses, The Curragh, Naas and Punchestown, within the confines of the county.

William Watson Ashe, known in racing circles as W.W. Ashe, kept racing stables at Narraghmore. His family was associated with horse breeding for about 400 years. A licence holder from 1925 to 1958, he turned out many good horses, both on the flat and over fences, including Finnure, Pointsman, Average, Fenlac Hill, Secret Service, Tokoroa, Steel Thread, Tír na nÓg and the One Eyed Gunner. He was recog-

SPORTS

nised by all as the best judge of a store horse in Ireland at the time. His father, also William Ashe, bred Ambush II, which won a maiden race at Punchestown and was later sold to the Prince of Wales. He won the English Grand National in 1900.

Willie Ashe farmed extensively, employing up to 30 people. He was interested in and supportive too of other sports, such as the local football team, who wore jerseys in his racing colours. It is on record that he was a member of the horse and pony race committee at the Crookstown Bazaar and fete in aid of parish funds in 1925. It is doubtful if even one horse grazes today on any of the 1,200 acres, that he once farmed.

The Flood family, who farm at Crookstown, Spratstown and at the Rocks, Grangecon have been involved in the horse racing business for generations.

It is recorded that Thomas Flood had two runners at the Kildare Hunt Point-to-Point in Mullaghmast in 1921. The horses were Rockberg and Turkish Girl and Mr. Flood's colours were green, with a white hoop and a pink cap. Francis, the best-known member of the family, was a very successful amateur rider for some 20 years, before taking out a licence to train in 1967. Success came quickly and in 1972 he saddled Glencarrig Lady to win the Cheltenham Gold Cup. Still a very successful trainer, having turned out two Irish Grand National winners in Garoupe and Ebony Jane, his all-weather gallop is just across the fence on the eastern bounds of the parish.

This article would not be complete without a mention of another great jockey, Willie Robinson, now resident in the parish for the past 12 years. He rode the famous Mill House to victory in the Gold Cup in 1963. He also partnered Team Spirit to win the English Grand National in 1964. Champion jockey in Ireland in 1958, he later went on to be a successful trainer. His greatest achievement was winning the 2000 Guineas with Kings Company in the early 1970s.

In years gone by many farmers kept a brood mare in the hope of getting a promising hunter, which they then broke in, riding to the hunt meets in the hope of attracting a customer from among the more wealthy followers. In more recent times many farmers in the parish kept a horse or two in training, some of them having a good share of success.

Surely the greatest success story in the parish during the 20th century was that of Frank Latham's Black Rath Stud, where the French horse Vulgan, rated as the best sire of chasers ever, stood for 18 years. Frank Latham bought Black Rath farm in 1944, as an addition to his training establishment in North County Dublin, where he still lived. He needed a manager to look after the farm so Michael Barry, a stud groom from Mallow, got the job. Barry suggested to Frank that he keep a stallion at Black Rath, but being more interested in training horses at the time, he was slow to make a change, but eventually agreed, and bought his first sire, Flamenco. Vulgan arrived in Black Rath in 1951. A small horse, he looked anything but the making of the champion sire he later proved to be. The stud housed the leading National Hunt sire for ten consecutive seasons, from 1965-66 to 1974-1975. During this period the title went to Vulgan eight times and twice to Escart III, who was also runner-up to his stable mate in the same period. Vulgan was champion sire 11 seasons in all. He produced three Grand National winners in Team Spirit (1964) Fionavon (1967) and Gay Trip (1970) a Cheltenham Gold Cup winner in The Dikler (1973), two Irish Grand National winners in Vulpine (1967) and Cole Bridge (1974). Escart sired L'Escargot, winner of two Gold Cups, as well as finishing 1st, 2nd and 3rd in his three Grand Nationals.

Other great stallions to stand at Black Rath, during those glory years that spanned four decades, were Figaro, Le Tricolore, Le Bavard, Star Signal, Torus, Bargello, Top of the World and Master Buck. It is worth noting that Dermot Whelan, stud groom at Black Rath for over 40 years, was a successful jockey in his early days, riding many winners for the Latham family before taking on responsibility for those valuable sires. The stud was a big asset to the community during those years, giving employment to up to ten local men, as well as providing a ready market for quality oats, hay and straw supplied, mainly, by local farmers.

Frank Latham received many awards during his lifetime, including the I.S.I.S. award for Bargello 1978, a presentation for outstanding achievement in National Hunt racing, the Champion Stallion award for Le Bavard in 1989 and also the Distinguished Service Award, presented by The Irish Thoroughbred Breeders Association. He died in February 1999, acknowledged by all as the most successful stud owner and manager of the century.

Fox hunting was also an important part of the racehorse industry, as horses had

Mr Frank Latham (R.I.P.)

SPORTS

Ebony Jane - Irish Grand National Winner

to qualify to compete in point-to-point races by hunting with a recognised pack of foxhounds. With three or four fox coverts in the parish the Kildare Fox Hounds were regular visitors to the area, meeting at Colbinstown, Calverstown, Narraghmore and Ballitore on a certain day each week. Spratstown was probably the best-known covert. It was in the care of the Nolan family for generations. Billy Nolan, Snr, took great pride in having a good fox in residence when the foxhounds called following the Thursday meet in Colbinstown and it would be unthinkable and a great letdown for him if his covert was to be drawn blank.

Many young people in the area have been involved with the Kildare Hunt Pony Club down the years under the watchful eye of Miss Pamela O'Mahony. It was common enough to see some ten or 12 children start out each morning exercising their ponies. Those young people benefited immensely in later life from the discipline and training which they received from being involved with the club. The farrier or blacksmith was an important part of the horseracing business, being in big demand all year round. Apart from the racing stables the farrier also got plenty of work from all the local farmers in the pre-tractor era. The Dowlings, Ballbarney, were probably the best-known farriers in the locality. They have been in business since the late Joe Dowling, Snr, took over from his uncle, John Winters, who had been shoeing horses since the early 1900s. Joe Dowling's sons carried on the tradition, shoeing horses all over south Kildare and into counties Wicklow and Laois.

The Kildare Hunt staged several point-to-point meets in the parish down through the years; the first recorded one was at Mullaghmast on Tuesday, March 29, 1921. There were five races on the card. Names listed among the owners were Flood, Masterson, Dunny, Byrne and Mc Dermott, probably all local farmers.

Point-to-point meets were held over a notoriously difficult course at Lipstown near Narraghmore for four or five years, starting in 1948. In recent times the hunt has found a regular home for the event at Punchestown which, in a way, is a pity as those events brought excitement and activity to rural communities. It can be truthfully said that the Parish of Narraghmore has made its mark in the field of horseracing and hunting down through the years.

SPORTS

MILL CELTIC

By Kevin Leigh

Mill Celtic was founded in 1988. The club was known as Ballitore FC up until 1992 and in those early days teams were entered in the Carlow and District League. Over the years a number of titles have been won and milestones reached. In 1992 Mill Celtic won the Carlow area of the FAI Junior Cup which meant the team reached the last 16 in the whole country.

The club won the John Farrell Counties Cup in 1995 beating Charleville Athletic from Tullamore but there was some disappointment that same year when Celtic was beaten in the Sheerin Cup final at Tolka Park. The club was beaten twice in the Counties Cup in recent years, in 1996 and 1998. Ironically it was the same opposition on both occasions. In 1996 Killa Villa won after a penalty shoot-out while they won 2-0 at the end of normal time two years later.

A number of local people from the Ballitore area have worked tirelessly for Mill Celtic down through the years. Kevin Leigh served as secretary for ten years and his wife Marian served as treasurer for a number of years. James Mackey (Snr) and Jim Kirwan were two other towers of strength in the success of the club and one other person who has to be mentioned is the late Ollie Cullen - a true martyr for the cause.

The current chairman is John Flood while Fiona Corcoran serves as secretary. Danny Mackey is the manager and Kathleen Corcoran is the treasurer. The club plays on Kildare County Council grounds at Mill Lane in Ballitore - hence the name "Mill Celtic". At the present time Mill Celtic play in the Kildare and District Soccer League in which they have won three different cups.

Kevin Leigh (Secretary) and Tony Nolan (Captain) with The Counties Cup in 1995

SPORTS

MILL CELTIC (1989 TEAM) WITH DIVISION ONE AND LEAGUE CUPS

*Back Row: Peter Daly, Tom Cullen, Liam Nolan, Mick Barrett, James Mackey, Jim Mackey, Danny Mackey, Sean Timmons, Kevin Leigh.
Front Row: James Mackey, Tom Mackey, Tony Nolan, Mick Donegan, Ronnie Mackey, Pat Mackey, Mick Enright, Ollie Lambe.*

Narraghmore Football Team

Supplied by Billy and Tony Donovan

Oh boys come gather around me and
listen to me here
About your local football team just
formed up last year
We haven't been the champions yet,
and we can only say
To behold us co. champions in
Newbridge park some day.

John McLoughlin is our keeper
and he is very sure,
Full back is Andy Dempsey,
on the left is Christy Moore
Ned Flood is on the right
and he is sure to clear
To Tommy Doyle of Burtown for whom
we will raise a cheer

Our centre half is Harry Ghent
and on the left is Dicer
Now there's a back line boys sure you
couldn't place them nicer
Our centre field O'Brien and Ging are a
pair both full of tricks
And when they get the ball they send it
through the sticks

Johnson Dempsey leads the attack
and on the left is Bill Blackburn
Jimmy Cantwell on the right is our
captain you must learn
Full forward Ginger Kenny,
on the left is Tommy Doyle
On the right is Johnny Ging
whose shot is sure to be in style
First sub P Ramsbottom
a young lad down from Leix
Next is PJ Kelly
who is sure to find a place

Louis Kelly from Fontstown
who has a place in store
And Tommy Flood complete the bunch
who come from Narraghmore
And now my friends you have them all
from goalman to the four
Just once again I'll call the men
Three cheers for Narraghmore

Narraghmore Parish and the GAA

By John Joe Walsh and Mai Finnegan

The Gaelic Athletic Association (GAA) was established in the billiards' room of Hayes Hotel in Thurles on November 1, 1884. Seven people were present at that first meeting, with Michael Cusack as the honorary secretary. Today the GAA reaches into every corner of the land and has its roots in every Irish parish.

Formed at a time when all forms of Irishness had been stamped out by political command, during a long period in which native language and native law were driven undergrounds, the culture of Gaelic games gave the Irish people a platform for self expression. Today, one million Irish people are members of the GAA, but this figure represents only a fraction of the Irish people who are touched by the games of hurling and football in their everyday lives. These great games have existed for many centuries. There is documented evidence of hurling games taking place in the 13th century and football was played in the 16th century but was very much a game of

Ballitore Football Team in the 1940s

rough and tumble, known as Caid. Today, more than ever, when our cities are getting bigger and our towns are expanding at an enormous rate, the GAA club has a huge part to play in the life of rural areas. Within the GAA club people can build on the energy that comes from pride of parish.

Since the GAA's inception in 1884 the parish of Narraghmore has been very active. Records show teams from the parish taking part in the Kildare championship as far back at the late 1890s. The Kildare records also show that Narraghmore people also played an active part in the administration of the GAA in County Kildare.

Ballitore O'Moore's were formed in 1888 and teams existed on and off in the village up to 1955. Other teams to have sprung up in the parish in the early years were; Brewel in 1889, Inchaquire in 1890, Ardellis in 1911 and Kilrush in 1920. Calverstown played Ballybarney in a friendly in Morrin's field in 1900 but apparently never played in the Kildare championship. Usk formed a team in 1949 and used Gorman's field as their home venue, but ceased to exist in 1950. King's Lawn was the pitch used by Narraghmore who were formed in 1934 and who brought the first silverware to the parish with the 1947 junior championship.

Bill Hendy's field was used by the Mullaghmast team which took part in the minor championships of 1956/'57 and '58.

St Ita's was briefly formed in 1966 and dissolved in February 1967. This was due to the fact that the St Laurence's club had been suspended in 1964 after a "fracas" in Geraldine Park in Athy during a championship match against Grangenolvin. The Kildare County Board dragged their feet on the issue, reinstated the club in June 1965 and re-imposed the suspension in August '65. Ironically St Laurence's were finally reinstated the week St Ita's was formed.

St Laurence's GFC was established on February 10, 1957. The two teams in the parish immediately prior to this were Ballitore and Narraghmore. Ballitore failed to enter a team in the 1955 or '56 Kildare championships and Narraghmore was competing but struggling for numbers. Fr Jim Kelly brought both teams together to form one club

Fr Jim Kelly
Founder of St. Laurence's GFC

and the name St Laurence's, the patron saint of the parish, was deemed to be acceptable to everybody. The committee formed on that day was: chairman, Fr Jim Kelly, CC; vice-chairman, Joe Dowling Snr; secretary, Billy Donovan/Sean Barrett; treasurer, Paddy Robinson; committee Paddy Doyle, Paddy Mackey, Davy Dillon, Charlie Lavin, Mick Lawler, Jack O'Connor, Denis Hughes and Billy Bevan.

Willie Ashe's field on the Wood Rd, Narraghmore, was the first pitch played on. Others used over the next 17 years were Kirwan's field at the back of the garda station, Bill Hendy's field in Mullaghmast, Kirwan's field at Abbey Row, Wall's field (now Jim Hannon's) opposite the garda station and Kirwan's field, which is now the graveyard in Crookstown.

In 1974 St Laurence's purchased six acres of land at Old Grange from the Land Commission and this has become the club's permanent home. 1981 saw the purchase of a mobile wooden structure which served both as dressing-rooms and meeting-room.

Showers and toilets were added in 1983/84. These served the club well until 1991 when a huge fund-raising drive was launched which culminated in the erection of the current permanent structure. The building includes dressing rooms, toilets and showers, storage rooms, referee's room and an upstairs function/meeting room with a small kitchen and ladies' and gents' toilets.

On a beautiful sunny day in May 1992

Mr Michael Lawler of Ballitore St Laurence's GFC - life president.

the new clubhouse was officially opened by the then President of the GAA, Peter Quinn. The day was marked by a challenge match between Kildare and Mayo. A huge crowd turned up to witness a Kildare victory. To add drama to the event Mr Quinn arrived and departed by helicopter. Croke Park had inadvertently booked him to open a new pitch in Ballyhale, County Kilkenny on the same afternoon!

The club continued to grow and, with an ever-increasing demand for the playing area, in 1996 it was decided to purchase an adjoining six acres of land from Bertie Stanley. Much hard work followed, moving of ditches, pipe draining, ploughing, levelling and seeding, plus the addition of two new dressing rooms to the back of the pavilion. The project was finally completed in 1999 and we had another official opening, this time performed by a Kildare man, Leinster Council Chairman, Seamus Aldridge.

Down provided the opposition on this occasion and unfortunately proved too strong for Kildare on the day with wee James McCartan taking the 'man of the match' award.

Always looking to progress the club installed floodlights on the new pitch in 1991 at a cost of €60,000. The lights have proved to be an enormous success and have allowed the grounds to remain active all year round.

On the playing fields it took St Laurence's a few years to break their duck but once this was achieved much success followed. At adult level the Junior B championship was captured in 1975, followed by the Junior A in 1978. An intermediate championship followed in 1980 and so the club joined the senior ranks in 1981. A very young St Laurence's team reached the county final in 1982 but were beaten by a star studded Sarsfields team. 1992 saw the club in its second county final, this time going down narrowly to Clane. The club's first title at senior level came with the capturing of the Senior League Div. 1 title, winning the Leinster Leader Cup, in 2000.

The club has worked hard at building up a very active under-age section and this is reflected in numerous successes down through the years.

With Castledermot on board the club won the minor championship in 1974. Another minor final was reached in 1980 but they were beaten by a Newbridge side that was an amalgamation of Sarsfields and Moorefield! The 1982 u21 championship final, between the same sides, resulted in a three-point defeat. The club won its only u16 county title in 1995. St Laurence's won the Kildare u14 Feile title in 2000 and went on to represent the county in the All Ireland u 14 Feile of that year. After a great run they were controversially beaten in the All Ireland semi-final by a Dublin team later proved to be playing numerous over-age players. Small consolation for the gallant St Laurence team.

The club fields 12 football teams in Kildare competitions, from adult to u8. In the last two years they have also fielded hurling teams at u12 and u14 level.

The club facilities are also used by the hugely successful camogie club who field teams from adult, down to under 10s.

The facilities of the club are used weekly for Irish figure dancing classes and set dancing and the club is delighted to be of assistance in the promotion of these great Irish pastimes. The local Humpty Dumpty Club for mothers and toddlers also use the clubhouse weekly.

You may notice there are practically no names mentioned in this brief account of the club's history. There are far too many people to mention who have given huge amounts of time and dedication over the last 46 years to enable St Laurence's GFC to become the vibrant progressive club that it is today and I fear I would leave names out.

The club has a membership of about 400 people at present and is in the early stages of further development with a planning application in for the erection of a sports hall/community centre at Old Grange. With the ever-increasing population in the parish the demands on the club to provide facilities for the youth of the area have never been greater. St Laurence's urgently needs an influx of new members with fresh ideas to assist in future development and in particular to get involved in the under age structure.

A survey of the GAA in 1890 carried out by the RIC for the State Office in Dublin Castle shows there were several GAA clubs in operation in the parish of Narraghmore.

Narraghmore Club Phadraig had 50 members. President, Thomas Hickey; treasurer, Thomas Waters; captain, James Hayden.

Inchaquire club had 25 members. President/treasurer, PJ Finn; secretary, Richard Archibold; captain, William Hickey.

Brewel Club had 50 members. President, Andrew Fay; secretary, Henry Fay; treasurer, John Cousins; captain, Charlie Flood. Ballitore O'Moore had 25 members. President, Pat Cullen; secretary/ treasurer, Pat Hendy; captain, William Fennell.

Michael Gorman is currently compiling a thorough history of the club and hopes to launch it in book form for the 50th anniversary of St Laurence's GFC in 2007.

ST. LAURENCE'S SENIOR CHAMPIONS 1992

Back (L To R): Mick Sullivan, Aidan Dempsey, Willie Keatley, Derek Lawler, Sean Ryan, Bernard Higgins, Johnny Ryan, Mick Fogarty
Front Row (L to R): Greg McLoughlin, P.J. Whelan, Seamus Ryan, Pat Keatley, Liam Miley, James Mackey, Richie Lawler.

SPORTS

Sport in the Parish

By Paddy Doyle

The first recorded attempt at organised athletics took place in the parish immediately after the Second World War in 1947. Brothers Billy and Paddy Nolan, together with the Owens brothers, Michael and Jack, all from Spratstown, and all now deceased, along with Billy Deay and James Delaney, formed a club known as the Millview Athletic and Cycling Club. Affiliated to the Kildare County Board under the governing body of the National Athletic and Cycling Association of Ireland, the club soon attracted young men from the locality and also drew members from Castledermot, Kilkea, Calverstown, Dunlavin and Moone. At that time cycle racing, both on grass and on the road, was very popular in rural areas, so the club soon had a strong team of runners and cyclists.

Over the following years the club enjoyed considerable success in both track and field and cross-country events within the county and beyond. Names like Denis Hughes, Arthur Lawler, Nicholas Donohue, James Delaney, Barney Deay, Paddy Doyle, Michael Humphries, Tony and Brendan Murphy and Jim Bryan, were constantly making the headlines, while cyclists like the Owens brothers, Billy Nolan, Dan O'Rourke and the late Patsy Doyle were the most prominent. The club remained active until 1953 when a combination of emigration and work commitments led to its demise.

A fresh start was made some years later with Joe Delaney, a younger brother of the founding member James, at the helm. This group was even more successful than the previous one. The revived club soon made its mark at county and regional level right up until 1976 when it was disbanded again. During that time men like Harry Coates, Joe Donovan, John O'Brien, Joe Delaney, Joe Foley, John O'Toole, John Moore, Tommy Byrne and Joe Lanigan wore the club colours with distinction in both track and field and cross-country competition.

In 1978 a few parents, whose children had become involved in Community Games in the county, came together to form a juvenile athletics club. Foremost among them were the afore mentioned Joe Delaney, his wife Sheila, Peter and Mary Kelly with Theresa Byrne and Mary McNamee. The club was known as Crookstown Athletic Club and was affiliated to the governing body BLE. It was obvious from the rapid growth in numbers over a short period that the timing of the establishment of the club could not have been better. A senior section was formed in 1981 and the club then became known as Crookstown Millview Athletic Club, the name it still retains today. An eight-acre field at the Pike Bridge was purchased in 1982, giving the club the honour of being the first athletic club in the county to own its own grounds. Rapid progress was made in competition, both at senior and juvenile level, with the result that the club won the trophy for best club in the county in 1984. This feat was repeated in 1986, along with another major achievement, that of winning the boys under 15 and under 16 club cross-country titles at national level. The 1980s could be described as the golden years for the club with athletes winning national titles at juvenile, junior, senior and veteran levels.

Sunday, July 15, 1987 was a gala day for the club when the eight-lane track at the Pike Bridge was officially opened. Br Cutbert Nolan, along with Tony Darcy, Leinster Secretary, who paid tribute to the club on its great achievement, cut the tape.

The 1990s brought along a whole new group of athletes who continued to keep the club to the forefront, winning national titles at all grades.

And so into the new millennium with new blood being infused at both committee and competition level, the future for the club looks bright indeed. The athletic grounds at Pike Bridge are a monument to the many people who so generously supported the project, and to the commitment and dedication of those involved in its development.

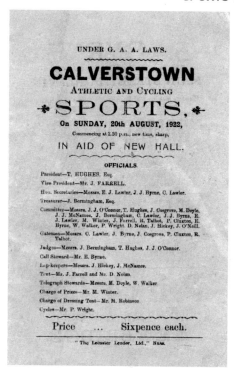

An early Leinster Leader (1922) leaflet promoting an athletic event.

Brother Cuthbert Nolan opens the new track in 1987.

SPORTS

ALL IRELAND CROSS COUNTRY CHAMPIONS 1987-1988

Back row: Colin Ryan, Fabian Flood, Mike Fox (Coach)
Front row: Paul Plewman, Derek Mackey, Wayne Logan

SPORTS

1979 ATHLETIC CLUB COMMITTEE

Front Row: Mary Delaney, Mary Kelly, Peter Kelly, Bridie Nolan, Nellie McDonnell
Back Row: Broda Leigh, Charlie Lavin, Teresa Byrne, Joe Delaney, Sheila Delaney, Paddy Doyle.

SPORTS

St Laurence's Golf Society

By Barry Kelly

The society began at an informal meeting in what was to become the 'clubhouse', Kelly's of Narraghmore. Present on that night in November 1995 were Mick Forman, Paddy Murphy, Barry Kelly, Sean Ryan and Willie Keatley. Barry Kelly wondered if the football club had thought about forming a golf society in the parish. This seemed to be a good idea as many of the players and officials had taken up playing golf. At that time few of them would have been GUI members so this would give them a chance to compete using handicaps.

Following the meeting a committee was formed: Barry Kelly, secretary and PRO; Tom Mulligan, handicap secretary; Sean Ryan, treasurer; Willie Keatley, captain. Also on the committee were Mick Gorman, Pierce Maher, Paddy Murphy and Tony McCabe. From the start it was a mixed society with men and women competing with one another. The first official outing took place in Kileen Golf Club with JJ Walsh, club chairman, teeing off the society.

In their first full year, 1996, the society held 12 outings with 25-30 of the full membership of 40 playing each time. The first official AGM took place at the end of that year. The society continues to go from strength to strength, both on a social and fundraising level. Membership has risen to 90 in 2003. People have formed great friendships and enjoyed great rivalry and comradeship, both at home and abroad. The society has also run fundraisers for the parish and football club.

The committee in 2003 is Tom Kelly, president; Paddy Lawlor, captain; Willie Keatley, secretary; Liam Mirby, treasurer; Nora P Walsh, PRO; Sean Ryan, handicap secretary; Committee, Dermot Kelly, Barry Kelly, Barry Browne, David Gray, Paul Byrne and Kay Kirby.

PHOTOS FROM THE ARCHIVES

1. Joy and James Cullen and Delia Lavin.
2. Dan Doyle, Carmel, Paddy, Andy and Rosanne Wright
3. Nan Ward and Willie Doyle.
4. Willie, Patrick, Dominic, Patricia and Deirdre Keatley.
5. Betty and Charlie Lavin
6. Margaret Ging and Nan and Rose Ward
7. Holy Communion class Ballymount NS 1959.
8. Out and about in Ballitore.
9. John O'Toole, Pat O'Toole, Charlie O'Toole, Sonny Flood, R McParland and Bridget O'Toole at Punchestown Races circa 1954.

Enjoying the haymaking.

A sunny Sunday afternoon

Bringing home the corn with Tony McNamee on board

The wedding dinner of Tony McNamee's parents

Mrs Mildred Ashe receiving the Ladies Cup from Mrs Madeline Shirley at Punchestown c 1950. Photo courtesy of the Irish Times.

AWARD WINNERS AT THE ATHLETIC CLUB IN 1984.

Front row. P. Byrne, ? Byrne, C. Byrne, D. O'Connor, E. Doyle, C. Haslam, A. Tallon.
Second row. R. Mackey, P. Flood, E. Hayden, D. Mackey, M. Hennessy,
N. Hennessy, M. Flood, V. Lawler, L. Byrne.
Third row. C. Mulhall, F. Farrell, B. Moore, D. Plewman,
F. Flood, J. Lawler, P. Plewman, S. Moore, L. Hayes.
Back row. V. Farrell, M. Kenny, A.Byrne, Y. Doyle, C. O'Halloran,
B. Conlan, A. Mulhall, Q. Nolan, A. Kelly and S. Fleming.

Rush hour in Balltore village!

Esther Doyle and Eileen Ghent were pictured at a Narraghmore/Ballytore Senior Citizens Christmas Party in Kelly's of Narraghmore.
Photo by Michael O'Rourke.

Enjoying the Narraghmore/Ballytore Senior Citizens Christmas Party in Kelly's of Narraghmore were Margaret Ryan, Mary-Anne Lawlor and Agnes Donovan.
Photo by Michael O'Rourke.

Smiling our way from the Narraghmore/Ballytore Senior Citizens Christmas Party in Kelly's of Narraghmore were Martha Power, Rita Mooney and Bea Hendy.
Photo by Michael O'Rourke.

Birdie Martin, Angela Swayne and Maureen Cullen were pictured at the Narraghmore/Ballytore Senior Citizens Christmas Party in Kelly's of Narraghmore.
Photo by Michael O'Rourke.

List of Contributors

Lorraine Callaghan
Willie Deacon
Michael Delaney
Billy Donovan
John Donovan
Tony Donovan
Paddy Doyle
Matt Doyle
Patricia Doyle
John Duffy
Pat Dunne
Mai Finnegan
Andrew Forrest
Carmel Gleeson
Joe Hickey
Hilary Healy
Christopher Heffernan
Philip Hendy
Denis Hughes
Barry Kelly
Representatives of Willie Kelly
Kevin Leigh
Kathleen Livingston
Bill Mackey
Mary Malone
Pauline Mooney
Mary McNamee
Pat O'Connor
John Joe Walsh
John Whelan
Sheila Whelan
Naomi White
Mark Wright

We wish to acknowledge the support of the following

Kildare European Leader II Teoranta
Pat Kelly Kelland Homes
Paddy Doyle
John Duffy
Seamus Byrne
Mary McNamee
Eileen Gorman
June Doyle
Sheila And Larry Whelan
Bernard Berney
Tom and Teresa Byrne
Mrs Iris Latham
John McNamee
Eddie and Ann Kearney
Matt and Patricia Doyle
P&M Print Athy
Duffey Bros Plumbing
Crookstown Tyre and Batteries Ltd
Leinster Marts Kilcullen
Sheila Heydon Hughes
Denis Hughes
Inchaquire Industries
St. Laurences GFC
St. Laurence's Golf Society
St. Laurence's Camogie Club

Ballytore Gun Club
Liffey Mills Athy
Corgan Construction Ltd
Kelly of Narraghmore
Therese Gorman 'Primrose Dell'
King Oil Athy
Elizabeth Hickey and Family
Cill Dara Oil
Joe Hickey
Brian Mc Parland
Cora Crampton
Glanbia Ballytore
Kilcullen Lions Club
Carmel Gleeson
John Dunne Construction
J P Quinn Building Contractor
Mary Anne Lawler
Mary Mc Loughlin
Ann Gorman
Nora Tallon
Mary Kelly
Rose Heffernan
Crookstown Millview Athletic Club
Betty Hughes
Narraghmore Credit Union

*We apologise in advance for any omissions or failure
to acknoweldge anyone who supported us.*

Narraghmore Local History Group 2003

Chairperson - Seamus Byrne, (retired farmer). Formerly involved with Ballitore Game Club and Irish dancing.

Secretary - Mary McNamee, (retired postmistress). Secretary Calvertstown Tidy Towns. Member of Scribblers Inc., Newbridge.

Assistant Secretary - Patricia Keatley, Engaged in farmhouse accommodation. Regional finalist Farmhouse of the Year 2003. Former camogie star, now coaches St Laurence's under age players. Co-organiser of the book launch.

Treasurer - Carmel Gleeson, Principal Crookstown National School. Interests include bridge, set dancing and playing music.

PRO: Paddy Doyle, (retired farmer and former sales rep for Avonmore). Founding member Crookstown-Millview Athletic Club and funding member of Narraghmore Whist Club, former star athlete and finalist Kildare Person of the Year 2003.

John Duffy, Farmer. This book was the brain child of John Duffy. Over the past few years John commissioned and compiled most of the articles with a view to publishing a local history book.

Sheila Whelan, Co-organiser of the book launch. Sheila is involved in Montessori teaching and is a member of Crookstown Liturgy Group and involved in parish fundraising.

Anne O'Reilly, Anne is a national school teacher and artist and did the painting for the cover 'Griese river at Ballitore Mill'.

The Griese Valley & Beyond

A PHOTOGRAPHIC COLLECTION

2003
Ballitore's Post-Mistress Lily O'Mara at her office counter

.....while Husband Tommy keeps and eye on the shop

St. Laurence's school - Rembrandts in training

School's out for Summer!. 3rd Class June 1998

Kids playing in Ballitore Library

Izelle Byrne with her pet cat 2003

BALLITORE 1986 - FESTIVAL DANCERS

Michael Maher

Natasha Murphy enjoying the sand

Aoifa, Natasha, Kayleigh and Ciara having fun

Seamus Buggle brings "Oisín's" double to visit the children in Calverstown

Blackrath Castle

The Old Post Office - Calverstown

Griesebank House and Old Mill

The Old Quaker Library - Ballitore

The Millennium Walk Gang
Brenda Mooney, Laura Mooney, Helen Mooney,
Laura Whelan and Larry Whelan

Millennium Walkers:
John Grufferty, Kathleen Grufferty, Kay Lawlor, Emma Grufferty,
Bridie Corrigan and Dermot Lawlor

Delia Lavin of Mayo (age 84) - 2003
One of the last surviving migrants from Mayo.

circa 1983
Batty (R.I.P) and Kathleen Kelly

Kathleen Kelly
and Annie Wright

Edward and Marie O'Mara in Fatima 2003

Betty Hughes and Mary McNamee in Fatima 2003

*Seamus Byrne, Denis Hughes, Pat Hughes (R.I.P.)
at the livestock mart in Kilcullen*

*All Ireland Relay Team 1991
At back: Mary Doyle - coach
A. O' Flaherty, N. Glynn, T. Hickey, D. Cosgove*

*All Ireland Winners 1995
Bridget and Pat Doyle*

*Louise Keatley
All Ireland Cross Country
Champion U11 2000*

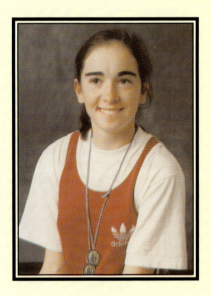

*Lynette Aspel
All Ireland Champion 800m &
1500m 1994*

St Laurence's Senior County Champions Ten in a Row - 1994 - 2003

Back Row (L to R): Manager - Karen Kelly, Elaine Miley, Naomi Treacy, Carol Nolan, Aisling Treacy, Roisin Walsh, Melanie Treacy, Margaret Butterfield, Deloris Browne, Susann Keatley, Selector - Margaret Sexton

Front Row: (L to R): Roxanne Treacy, Realtin Treacy, Ruth Treacy (capt), Ciara Tallon, Pamela Donovan, Niamh Breen, Liz O'Donohue Byrne, Lily Bowden, Mascot - Dearbhla Byrne

Co. Kildare Cross Country Champions 1985
Paddy Doyle (Chairman), Rita Nolan, Aisling Berney, Deirdre Keatley, Marie Kelly, Harry Mulhall

St Laurence's Leinster Leader Cup Winners 2000

"I can now read my newspaper in comfort", says Tony McNamee at the kitchen table which has been home to the History Group leading up to publication of this book.